EFFORT, OPPORTUNITY,
AND WEALTH

EFFORT, OPPORTUNITY, AND WEALTH

Julian L. Simon

Basil Blackwell

British Library Cataloguing in Publication Data

Simon, Julian L.
  Effort, opportunity, and wealth.
  1. Economic development   2. Achievement
  motivation
  I. Title
  330.9   HD82

  ISBN 0–631–14428–5

Library of Congress Cataloging in Publication Data

Simon, Julian Lincoln, 1932–
  Effort, opportunity, and wealth.

  Includes index.
  1. Entrepreneur.   2. Struggle – Economic aspects.
  3. Competition.   4. Wealth.   I. Title.
  HB615.S55   1987   330.1   86–17644
  ISBN 0–631–14428–5

Typeset in 11 on 13 pt Ehrhardt
by Opus, Oxford
Printed in the USA

Contents

Acknowledgements

I appreciate useful comments on earlier drafts by Daniel Hamermesh, Dieter Helm, Nathaniel Leff, Edwin A. Locke, Shlomo Maital, David Osterfeld, John Pencavel, Walter Primeaux, Salim Rashid, Edward Rice, John P. Robinson, James Smith, and Aaron Wildavsky. I benefited from the opportunity to discuss some of this material at the Austrian Seminar at New York University.

Stephen Moore provided excellent research assistance of many sorts. The Word Processing Center at the College of Commerce at the University of Illinois, headed by Carol Halliday, did a superb job typing the various chunks of the manuscript. And Helen Demarest put the finishing touches to the typescript with her usual good cheer, good sense, and dedication to the job. Thank you all.

Julian L. Simon

A Personal Note

Perhaps some words about the author's feelings toward this book are appropriate – more so than in most economics writing – because this book treats people as beings with feeling, and considers the economic implications of feeling, rather than dealing with the more mechanical aspects of humans as economic actors.

Effort – speaking now in an idiom different from the formal analysis that is the heart of this book – depends upon what we call the human will. And the human will flows from what many of us would call the human spirit. This human spirit, we are willing to say when we are not talking economics, is the well-spring of the creative impulse and the creative capacity. These, in turn, are the source of advance in civilization, which consists of contributions to our treasury of art as well as to progress in technical knowledge and consequent gains in the standard of living. The first impulse for this book, well before I even began to grope for the central analytical idea, came after looking at the work of my friend, Aristides Demetrios, who makes great sculpture, and after talking with him about the life force and the thought that goes into his work.

The role in civilization's advance of inventors, artists, and entrepreneurs is obvious. But what contribution can economics and economists make? It seems to me that economists – along with other social scientists and historians – can contribute by learning about the structure of economy and society which will best promote the process of progress, so that lawmakers and government servants in turn can bring about these conditions. We already know that this structure includes providing the freedom from unnecessary constraints so that creative individuals and organizations will dream bold dreams of awesome projects, and offering incentives that will bring forth their greatest efforts to realize their dreams, while not choking off or misdirecting their creative efforts by confiscating their gains or preventing their freewheeling operations in the name of preventing negative externalities; consider Hong Kong and Tanzania. A benign structure also includes allowing for sufficient competition among private organizations, and also among public organizations such as municipalities and states, to test a variety of innovations and to winnow out the best among them; such pluralism in Europe, the historians have recently reported, is a likely cause of the surge in progress that took place there but not in China or India. And it includes organizing and co-ordinating the large social projects, such as space exploration, which may not be done early enough by individuals without the encouragement of government, while not wasting the resources of society in vast vain boondoggles. The experiences of the past are the materials to which we can apply the tools of systematic evaluation to sort out the conditions of progress from the conditions of stagnation.

I hope that this book helps in the work.

1
Introduction

All of us act as if the concept of effort has meaning and is useful. We believe that the amount of effort exerted differs among people and depends upon the circumstances. In common speech and in popular writing we use effort to help explain the outcome in many activities such as sports, school, and work. We feel our own exertions of effort in our minds and in our bodies, both while exerting the effort and afterwards. Yet economists have not heretofore taken account of variations in effort in analyses of economic phenomena.

This short book postulates that the amount of effort which a person will exert depends upon two factors: (a) the opportunity that the person perceives to earn additional income, and (b) the person's 'need' for additional income as measured by the person's wealth. Of course the effort also depends upon a host of other factors stemming from nature, nurture, and the current environment. But those other factors are considered extraneous here. My aim is not to 'explain' the effort exerted by individuals, but rather to understand the effect of economic variables. To that end, the book focuses upon only wealth, opportunity, and the relationship between them, except for a few forays outside of economic behaviour to see how far the analysis can be extended fruitfully.

More particularly, the book postulates that the amount of effort (drive) is a function of the arithmetic difference between wealth with and without the opportunity in question, considered relative to the person's current wealth. This central concept of Drive–Effort has close links to the psychologist's concept of the Just Noticeable

Difference (JND) and to the economist's concept of diminishing marginal utility.

This Drive–Effort formulation can serve as a precise definition of the concept of incentive.

The concept of wealth refers to what one can purchase with one's present assets. The concept of opportunity refers to the additional assets one can obtain by accepting the alternative under discussion.

Various types of evidence are offered in support of this postulation. No piece of evidence by itself is strong enough, or sufficiently direct, to constitute full confirmation. But I hope that the totality of the evidence makes a solid case that the Drive–Effort formulation is sufficiently supported so that it seems reasonable as well as useful.

Effort is manifested both in the *amount of time* that a person works, and in the *intensity* with which a person exerts himself or herself during the time devoted to work. The two aspects of effort are linked in being substitute methods for achieving the same end; a person may work harder, or for longer, or both, in order to finish the job.

Intensity is the more interesting and perhaps the more important aspect of effort. Regrettably, however, work time is easier to discuss because there are more extant relevant data, and also because economic theory has given it more attention. I hope that these circumstances do not influence the reader to dwell less on the intensity of work effort than on its extent, however.

After setting forth the intellectual underpinning of the effort concept, and a formal statement of it, the book proceeds to apply the central idea to a variety of situations. One purpose of the applications is to demonstrate the power and versatility of this analytic tool. A second purpose is to offer substantive hypotheses about a variety of economic circumstances that are interesting in themselves, ranging from an explanation of why competition may lead to greater vigour in firms' activity than does monopoly in chapter 6, to a suggested explanation for the decline of empires in chapter 8.

The analysis of behaviour in monopoly compared with that in duopoly, which should generalize to the question of how the presence of competitors affects the vigour of competition among firms, is the analytic centrepiece of the book because it demonstrates in detail the use of the method. Economists have heretofore taken for granted that the presence of competitors induces firms to compete more vigorously, but the matter has gone unexplained in systematic and formal fashion; the outcome turns out to be more complex and less clear-cut than expected.

The analysis of monopolistic versus duopolistic behaviour hinges on an objective specification of incentive, a concept central to economic thinking which, upon inspection, is seen to be ambiguous, and is commonly used in conflicting fashions. The concept of Drive–Effort is the other side of the coin from the concept of incentive, and is offered as an operational and objective definition of it.

Economic analysis usually assumes that all the decision units are identical. Among the few exceptions to this rule are differences in natural resource endowment, differences in consumer tastes that lead to exchange, differences in risk preference, and Engel-curve-type consumption systems. This assumption of homogeneity of economic agents is very convenient theoretically. By discussing the behaviour of the 'representative' firm or consumer as it interacts with similar firms or consumers, the standard analysis can arrive at an equilibrium without the complications which would arise if the interacting units were assumed to differ on such dimensions as size, assets, knowledge, and market share.

For some purposes, however, the assumption of homogeneity does not serve well. The external disequilibria that induce profit-seeking economic activity, and the internal conditions that lead firms and individuals to respond to these disequilibria, often depend upon differences in the abilities of the competing firms and individuals caused by prior experiences, as well as by differences in such characteristics as size. Austrian economists, especially Hayek, have emphasized that these differences have an important effect upon the nature of competition. Arrow's analysis of organizations and their behaviour takes a similar point of view (1974). Industrial-organization theorizing about such phenomena as price leadership and price umbrellas also exemplifies analysis that necessarily deals head-on with such differences among firms. Recently, such concepts as implicit contract, specific human capital, and firm-specific effects have arisen to deal with differences among business units. These concepts point in the same general direction as does this book. But such departures from the assumption of uniformity are still only a small part of economic thinking.

One of the most important internal conditions in which firms and individuals differ is the information which they possess about markets and the business environment. This is the Austrians' central point; they emphasize its far-reaching consequences for business behaviour and for the development of an orderly economic structure. Different states of information about economic opportunities necessarily lead to differences in Drive–Effort, though the point will not be developed here. One would like to know (a) the extent to which such differences in information states relate to actual effort expended, an interesting empirical question; and (b) how wealth, and the Drive–Effort Measure that will be defined later, affect people's search for information about disequilibria and economic opportunities. Both these questions must mostly be left for the future, however.

Please understand that the differences among firms and individuals are not being analysed here because they are interesting in their own right. Rather, these differences in internal conditions are employed to explain systematically such differences in economic behaviour and economic outcomes as, for example, why one nation waxes richer while another wanes poorer, and why firms exert different amounts of effort when there is competition than when there is monopoly.

Better understanding of the influence of one's economic circumstances upon one's economic behaviour may help us understand a variety of interesting and important questions such as:

1 Why do some nations and groups of people work longer hours than others? The answers 'Because they are poorer' and 'Because they have a value for hard work' are inadequate; though such statements may be suggestive, they are not easily rendered precise in terms of economic theory.

2 Why have the once richest nations been surpassed in wealth by other nations that were formerly less rich? Answers citing wars and political personalities may be strengthened by consideration of economic conditions and consequent changes in effort.

3 Why has economic development tended to take place in temperate climes? The answer 'Because there is enough but not too much challenge' may have much truth in it, but cannot easily be co-ordinated with other economic propositions.

4 How does one sensibly think about a situation such as that of the Crow Indians who own 'huge coal reserves' and also have 'an unemployment rate approaching 70%'?[1] Talk about 'lack

of jobs' obviously is an incomplete explanation at best; before the white people came, there were no 'jobs' at all in the modern sense, and no one worried about a high unemployment rate or idleness.

A pressing practical question upon which these chapters bear is whether, in the context of the United States at present, changes in the opportunity structure of taxes, regulations, and economic institutions will 'get this country going again'.[2] Does, or does not, some combination of the wealth level, the educational system, and our values and aspirations influence people's work propensities in such fashion that no conceivable changes in the opportunity structure could elicit the enterprise, hard work, and ingenuity that Americans exhibited in the past? Another pressing question, always with us, concerns the trade-off between giving welfare and providing incentive to work.

The viewpoint of this book may be compared with Schultz's view of the related topic of entrepreneurship (1980), wherein the key element is a dimension of human capital of the same order as education and physical strength, and with Kirzner's view of entrepreneurship (1985) wherein the activity with which he is concerned is 'costless'. My viewpoint contrasts particularly sharply with Becker's view of effort, to be discussed in chapter 3, wherein the hours-worked aspect of effort is an allocation decision at the expense of leisure, taken from a total fixed quantity of available time, and wherein the intensity aspect of effort is thought of in a similar fashion.

Unlike Schultz and Becker, my interest here is in the aspects of human capital which are *unlike* physical capital. A person who has been trained to shovel dirt efficiently has much in common with a post hole digger, and a person who has been trained to draw maps reliably has much in common with a computer that does a similar task. But a machine does not vary its output of dirt or maps or new ideas in response to worries about losing its job because of working too slowly, or in response to hopes that a new enterprise will succeed and put the children through college. It is motivation, imagination, ethical decisions, altruism, character, courage, perception, and the like that are the subject of this book. These characteristics of persons and groups which depend upon circumstances that do not affect a machine, but which do affect the course of civilization, are the subject of interest here.

Though the feeling aspect of effort is at the heart of the mechanism, the subject-matter is completely economic. Both the determinants of effort, and the consequences of it that are discussed here, are wholly material and objective, that is, economic in magnitude. This also is in contrast to Becker's approach, a main objective of which is an improvement in our understanding of the individual, that is, an advance in psychology.

The subject of risk is perhaps the closest analogy in the current domain of economics. Though we talk about a *taste* for risk-bearing, it is really the *feeling* of fear that influences a person to choose a portfolio with a smaller amount of risk and a lower expected value than a riskier portfolio with a higher expected value. And as with my treatment of effort, in the analysis of risk no fixed endowment is postulated within which the feeling toward risk is traded off against another element.

Chapters 2 and 3 of the book discuss the economic literature on optimization with respect to various inputs for production and consumption – purchased inputs, one's own time à la Becker, and effort. An objective definition of Drive–Effort as a function of wealth and economic opportunity – which also provides a definition of 'incentive' – is put forth in chapter 4. That discussion shows, I believe, that the analysis of expended effort usefully supplements the analysis of time allocation and of profit maximization in understanding important economic behaviour and outcomes.

Chapter 5 reviews data relevant to the hypothesis, and describes some tests that could falsify it. Chapter 6 follows with the formal analysis of monopoly versus duopoly. Chapter 7 discusses a variety of situations which the concept of Drive–Effort may help explain. These situations are not analysed at length or in depth, unlike the analysis of monopoly–duopoly in chapter 6; rather, the brief discussion of each situation in chapter 7 is intended only to be suggestive, and the basis of possible future analysis. Chapter 8 discusses various policy implications of Drive–Effort analysis.

A brief summary, chapter 9, ends the book.

Notes

1 *Wall Street Journal*, 31 January 1984.
2 This was first written in 1983, when that question seemed especially pressing.

2

Context and Background

Introduction to Effort as an
Economic Variable

This work postulates that wealth, opportunity, and the relationship between them constitute a key influence on the economic behaviour of individuals and nations, and largely determine whether people accept or reject economic opportunities.

The relative importance of material incentives in determining human activity has always been the subject of large disagreement. Varying views on the issue have affected many practical aspects of life; for example, the practice of labour relations in the United States has been strongly influenced by the Hawthorne experiment, which purportedly showed that factors other than wages explain much of the variation in productivity.[1] Views about the importance of material incentives, and reactions to the concept of 'economic man', also have affected attitudes toward various bodies of thought – for example, the distaste of many persons for classical economic theory which supposedly assumes (though it does not) that people aim only to acquire more money.

The need for an effort concept is often apparent in economic analysis. An illuminating example of how the absence of the effort concept affects analysis is seen in the context of foreign aid. According to the fundamental definition of economic welfare, a gift to a person increases that person's welfare because the gift increases the person's 'endowment', that is, the person's purchasing power. But even the best of ecomonists may be heard to say that giving food as foreign aid is usually bad. If the weather gives us more wheat, we are better off, but if we give the wheat to Mexico, they may be made worse off. What explains this apparent logical contradiction? In the case of market agriculture and a government-to-government gift, a satisfactory explanation can be framed in standard terms, though the explanation lacks the logical precision usually demanded of economics: reduction of the market price caused by the gift leads farmers to reduce agricultural activity, which causes reduction in physical and human investment, which will have bad effects after the aid has ended. The need for an effort concept is plainest if the aid goes to a subsistence farmer: the gift causes reduction in effort later when there is no aid by those least prepared to exert effort.[2]

Writers as various as Mandeville (1705/1962), Hume (1953), Marshall (1920, p. xv), McClelland (1961), Hoselitz (1960), Kristol (1978), Bell (1973), Gilder (1984), Novak (1982), and Maital (1982), with perhaps Schumpeter (1942/1950) and Weber (1923/1961) and various anthropologists in the background, argue that various elements in people's thinking which affect economic behaviour (aside from productive know-how) differ from individual to individual, from group to group, and from one situation to another.

Mandeville wrote:

> Man never exerts himself but when he is roused by his desires; while they lie dormant, and there is nothing to raise them, his excellence and abilities will be forever undiscovered, and the lumpish machine, without the influence of his passions, may be justly compared to a huge windmill without a breath of air.
> (Mandeville, 1705/1962, p. 120)

Bauer (1981) goes so far as to suggest that *only* institutions and the contents of people's minds matter economically, and physical circumstances are not important; he cites Hong Kong as his example. McClelland has even attempted to implement this general view with an experiment to alter the outlooks and motivations of a sample of Indian business men, and he observed (though the finding is controversial) important changes in their business behaviour as a consequence of the training that he gave them.

M. and R. Friedman write as follows about the effect of the pay-off upon the effort exerted:

> If Red Adair's income would be the same whether or not he performs the dangerous task of capping a runaway oil well, why

should he undertake the dangerous task? He might do so once, for the excitement. But would he make it his major activity? If your income will be the same whether you work hard or not, why should you work hard? Why should you make the effort to search out the buyer who values most highly what you have to sell if you will not get any benefit from doing so?

(Friedman and Friedman, 1980, p. 15)

In a discussion of economic policies – as distinct from a discussion of economic theory – economists typically suggest 'privatizing' economic activities and resources, and 'internalizing' costs, in order to provide 'incentive' for hard and diligent work. But the term 'incentive' invariably goes undefined; it is usually just a synonym for money, on the assumption that people prefer more to less purchasing power. No distinction is made among persons as to the motivating incentive power of a given sum of money; no method of measurement of incentive is offered.

When writing theory, however, most economists implicitly take the view that aspirations and motivations either do not differ much among groups and among periods of time, or else that aspirations and motivations are sufficiently flexible as to change almost immediately when the relevant economic conditions change.[3] De Allessi states as one characteristic of neo-classical theory that 'the entrepreneur's choice between income and leisure is independent of income' (1983, p. 65).

An example of this homogeneity assumption is found in Schultz's writing on entreprenurial activities:

The supply of services from these abilities depends upon the stock of a particular form of human capital at any point in time and on the costs and the rate at which the stock can be increased in response to the rewards derived from the services of these abilities. (Schultz, 1975, p. 834)

When economists discuss variations in work propensity, they often do so in a casual manner, in sharp contrast to the precision common in the treatment of standard economic concepts. Let us take Samuelson as an example; given that he received a Nobel prize for raising the level of economic analysis, this is no straw man being attacked. He is quoted as follows in explaining the 1970s slowing of productivity and growth: 'Mr. Samuelson thinks a key factor is the demise of the work ethic, a deterioration fostered by affluence and by a host of well-meaning, but excessive income support programs.'[4] The concept of 'work ethic' goes undefined in such discourse, and indeed has no place in contemporary economic theory.

Some writers have speculated that individual human qualities have become less important in the modern economy than they were in subsistence agriculture or early capitalism. Schumpeter, for example, wrote an entire chapter on 'The Obsolescence of the Entrepeneurial Function', saying:

> This social function is already losing importance and is bound to lose it at an accelerating rate in the future even if the economic process itself of which entrepreneurship was the prime mover went on unabated. For, on the one hand, it is much easier now than it has been in the past to do things that lie outside familiar routine – innovation itself is being reduced to routine. Techno-logical progress is increasingly becoming the business of teams of trained specialists who turn out what is required and make it work in predictable ways. The romance of earlier commercial adventure is rapidly wearing away, because so many more things can be strictly calculated that had of old to be visualized in a flash of genius.
>
> On the other hand, personality and will power must count for less in environments which have become accustomed to economic change – best instanced by an incessant stream of new consumers' and producers' goods – and which, instead of resisting, accept it as a matter of course. The resistance which comes from interests threatened by an innovation in the productive process is not likely to die out as long as the capitalist order persists. It is, for instance, the great obstacle on the road toward mass production of cheap housing which presupposes radical mechanization and wholesale elimination of inefficient methods of work on the plot. But every other kind of resistance – the resistance, in particular, of consumers and producers to a new kind of thing because it is new – has well-nigh vanished already.
>
> Thus, economic progress tends to become depersonalized and automatized.   (Schumpeter 1942/1950, p. 325)

Lenin, too, assumed that accountants and clerks routinely carry out the important activities of business in machine-like fashion with entrepreneurial effort:

Accounting and control – these are the *chief* things necessary for the organizing and correct functioning of the *first phase* of communist society. *All* citizens are here transformed into hired employees of the state, which is made up of the armed workers. *All* citizens become employees and workers of *one* national state 'syndicate'. All that is required is that they should work equally, should regularly do their share of work, and should receive equal pay. The accounting and control necessary for this have been *simplified* by capitalism to the utmost, till they have become the extraordinarily simple operations of watching, recording and issuing receipts, within the reach of anybody who can read and write and knows the first four rules of arithmetic.

(Possony, 1966, p. 208; italics in original)

Marshall was a forceful counter-voice, emphasizing the primacy of a non-mechanical view of human nature for the purposes of the economist:

The main concern of economics is thus with human beings who are impelled, for good and evil, to change and progress. Fragmentary statical hypotheses are used as temporary auxiliaries to dynamical – or rather biological – conceptions: but the central idea of economics, even when its Foundations alone are under discussion, must be that of living force and movement. (Marshall, 1920, p. xv)

And Marshall explained the opposite tendency of the classical writers as follows:

For the sake of simplicity of argument, Ricardo and his followers often spoke as though they regarded man as a constant quantity . . . It caused them to speak of labour as a commodity without staying to throw themselves into the point of view of the workman; and without dwelling upon the allowances to be made for his human passions, his instincts and habits, his sympathies and antipathies, his class jealousies and class adhesiveness, his want of knowledge and of the opportunities for free and vigorous action. They therefore attributed to the forces of supply and demand a much more mechanical and regular action than is to be found in real life.   (Marshall, 1920, pp. 762–3)

The view of economic motivation and behaviour that underlies thinking has major policy implications for a nation, affecting narrowly-economic forecasts and expectations and plans, as well as decisions about how schooling and other institutions are to proceed.

Earlier Theory

It is a basic tenet of economic theory that if the potential reward is increased, businesses and individuals will supply more goods and services to the market. For analytic purposes, the market price is the central motivating element. Contrary to popular notion, however, this tenet does not mean that classical economics asserted that the drive for material goods is the main motive of human beings. Smith made clear that the regard of one's fellows is our most important motive. And before Smith, Mandeville put the matter as follows:

> The meanest wretch puts an inestimable value upon himself, and the highest wish of the ambitious man is to have all the world, as to that particular, of his opinion: so that the most insatiable thirst after fame that ever hero was inspired with was never more than an ungovernable greediness to engross the esteem and admiration of others in future ages as well as his own; and (what mortification soever this truth might be to the second thoughts of an Alexander or a Caesar) the great recompense in view, for which the most exalted minds have with so much alacrity sacrificed their quiet, health, sensual pleasures, and every inch of themselves, has never been anything else but the breath of man, the aerial coin of praise.
>
> (Mandeville, 1705/1962, p. 48)

Marshall pointed out that the opportunities for choosing a level of effort are greater than might be thought, and are chosen by mobility if no other way:

> ... there are scarcely any trades, in which the amount of exertion which he puts into his work is rigidly fixed. If he be not

able or willing to work up to the minimum standard that prevails where he is, he can generally find employment in another locality where the standard is lower; while the standard in each place is set by the general balancing of the advantages and disadvantages of various intensities of work by the industrial populations settled there. The cases therefore in which a man's individual volition has no part in determining the amount of work he does in a year, are as exceptional as the cases in which a man has to live in a house of a size widely different from that which he prefers, because there is none other available.
(Marshall, 1920, pp. 527–8)

Hicks (1932/1963) expanded the formal analytic apparatus to include the individual's desire for leisure as a second motivating element. This apparatus helps explain why an increase in the price of labour could sometimes lead to less rather than more labour being supplied by given individuals. (A section in chapter 5 aims to give new precision to the idea of the backward-bending supply curve of labour, using the central analytical mechanism of this book.)

Another theoretical improvement occurred when Fisher (1930) and Modigliani (1966) formalized the obvious fact that a person's wealth affects the person's decision about how much to save and how much to consume within a given period: more wealth, less saving out of income. They placed the saving-consumption decision in the context of the remaining segment of the person's lifetime, and they analysed the intended allocation of the person's assets over that period. Some writers, Feldstein (1974), for example, have discussed the work-versus-leisure decision in the same context, but I have not traced the intellectual history of that idea to its roots.

Earlier, Chayanov (1923/1966) formally modelled how differences in circumstances, such as different numbers of children, affect the work decisions of the subsistence farmer. His analysis, postulating particular indifference relationships between goods and leisure, fits the case of any working person having variable work opportunities. Similar theory was later reinvented by a number of writers including Mellor (1963) and Sen (1966).

Becker (1965; 1976) expanded the theory of economic motivation with a richer analysis of the relationships among wages, wealth, and work time. He introduced as a variable the time-intensivity of the various goods which additional income would buy, and he traced the effect of that variable upon the work–leisure decision. He also (1976) placed work and savings decisions in the context of the remainder of the life-cycle and the expected amounts of lifetime, wealth, and earning power. But Becker's main interest is not the effects of the individual's economic behaviour upon total economic production, but rather the individual's behaviour in general. The widening of the focus to include more than economic behaviour is seen in the title of Becker's 1976 book, *The Economic Approach to Human Behavior*. In contrast, a label for the present essay, playing upon Becker's title, might be *The Human Approach to Economic Behaviour*.

The analysis of risk as another aspect of motivation came into economic analysis mainly by way of von Neumann and Morgenstern (1947; Knight's earlier work, 1921/1965, did not enter formal theory). This theoretical strand seems at first to have the opposite implication from the Drive–Effort analysis offered here. If a new risky investment opportunity appears, the person with greater wealth will be more likely to invest a given sum of money than will the person of lesser wealth, because of differences in risk aversion. And if the opportunity requires work participation by the investor as well as capital, and if the rest of the individual's life cannot be rearranged for the moment but rather is properly treated as fixed, the richer person may be more likely to do the additional work that goes with the investment than the poorer person. But if the investment is primarily 'sweat equity', the poor person will be more likely to accept the opportunity. That is, though it is common to assert that the poor are more averse to risk than are the rich, and hence the utility function of the poor is more concave than that of the rich, this observation should be understood to refer only to monetary investments unconnected with time, effort, or bodily risk. For example, a poor person is more likely to volunteer for a particularly risky job than is a rich person. In such a situation the effect of wealth through risk works in the same direction as it does in other aspects of motivation; that is, it is consistent with the Drive–Effort analysis. And the analysis presented here would seem to be quite compatible with the observation of similar behaviour to risk measured as a *proportion* of wealth, for persons with different levels of wealth, as the literature shows.[5]

Leibenstein (1976, p. 7) emphasizes the importance of what he calls 'the effort decision'. Much of his discussion of the topic is helpful and interesting. But the effort concept discussed here is quite different from Leibenstein's concept. For Leibenstein, 'The effort–utility relation reflects an individual's personality' (p. 108), and he also mentions 'pressure' (including group relations) as an influence on effort; both have the drawbacks that they are not easily measurable for this sort of purpose, and are outside the set of ordinary economic variables. In contrast, the influences on effort in the framework presented here are entirely economic: initial wealth, and the size of earning opportunity, which are mostly objective and measurable. And the intensity of effort is similar to Becker's time input (1965) as an economic variable, though probably somewhat harder to measure in most cases. Moreover, Leibenstein suggests that for most people, additional effort 'has greater utility' in the range of low effort, and his function changes direction at higher effort. In contrast, it is implicit in the formulation used here that less effort is preferred to more effort.[6]

Hirschman builds his theory of responses to decline in firms, organizations, and states (1970) on the idea that as the firm's business drops off or an organization loses membership, 'revenues drop, membership declines, and management is impelled to search for ways and means to correct whatever faults have led to exit'. And when the customers or members 'express their dissatisfaction . . . the *voice option* . . . management once again engages in a search for the causes and possible cures of customers' and members' dissatisfaction'. He assumes that slack exists in organizations, as it does in economies and societies generally. The 'basic proposition' of his earlier book *The Strategy of Economic Development* (1958) was that 'development depends not so much in finding optimal combinations for given resources and factors of production as on calling forth and enlisting for development purposes resources and abilities that are hidden, scattered or badly utilized'. This is closely related to the concept of effort.

The concept of slack may not be the most happy one in this context, however. It suggests that persons 'ought' to be doing more than they do, and one need not see it that way. It also has the disadvantage of implying that there is a fixed limit on what the person can do. It might be better to see the matter as a continuous function like a cost curve, where at higher levels the cost of another unit of input becomes greater and greater. Just what must be paid for the input is murky, however. And perhaps it is that murkiness which makes inappropriate the usual profit-maximizing logic of economics which assumes that the inputs can be cleanly measured.

Pencavel made a valiant attempt to attract the attention of economists to variations in effort, noting that 'analytical work in economics of a more recent vintage has tended to ignore the intensity of work effort' (1977, p. 225), though managers treat the effort of their workforces as an important variable. But there has been no rush to heed his call.

Hall discussed systematic variation in effort over the business cycle as one of the implicit elements in the long-run wage contract. There is, he says, 'an implicit or explicit agreement that employees work harder when there is more work to do . . . Workers put in extra effort during booms and take it easy during slumps' (1980, pp. 93, 95). He ingeniously calculates the components of the (deviations from the trend of) changes in total output during the two contraction periods of 1970–1 and 1974–5, finding that decreased intensity of work effort caused 1.1 per cent change (out of 7.3 per cent total change), and decreased hours per worker caused another 2.6 per cent change. So decreased work effort accounted for more than half the change in total output. (The employment rate and the participation rate account for the rest.) And decreased work intensity – less output per hour – accounted for $1.1/7.3 = 15$ per cent of the change (p. 96).)

Change in opportunity accounts for the change in effort in Hall's analysis. The change in opportunity is at the level of the firm, and the effect is transmitted to the workers through the long-run wage bargain Hall is analysing. Opportunity is one of the two elements in the Drive–Effort Measure that is suggested in this book.

Social scientists other than economists have offered a variety of explanations for the amount of effort put forth. For example, Toynbee offered his challenge-and-response mechanism to explain various occasions in history when nations and groups have made exceptional efforts. However, the hypothesis of this book – that greater opportunity evokes greater effort – seems to run *exactly counter* to Toynbee's notion of challenge and response, which states that more severe conditions – that is, lesser opportunities – evoke greater drive:

We have ascertained that civilizations come to birth in environments that are unusually difficult and not unusually easy; and this had led us on to inquire whether or not this is an instance of some social law which may be expressed in the formula: 'the greater the challenge, the greater the stimulus'.

(Toynbee, 1962, p. 259)

Mixing together endowments and opportunities into the single independent variable 'challenge' accounts for Toynbee's confusing proposition. And indeed, many of the historical examples that Toynbee (p. 274) cites in support of his theory – Venice, Holland, and Switzerland, for example – fit more neatly with a theory using *both* opportunity and endowment as explanatory concepts than they do with Toynbee's combination variable 'challenge'.

McNeill (1963, pp. 56 ff) posits social instability, political fragmentation, market orientation, and openness to new ideas as the causes of Europe showing intellectual and physical vigour not seen in Asia in centuries past. Hagen (1962) and others have put forth a variety of psychological factors (some related to self-selection), including discrimination and social derogation, as causes of immigrants working harder than natives. Weber (1923/1961) and other sociologists have suggested that values – such as the 'Protestant ethic', or the Confucian family relationships and child training – influence aspirations and work behaviour. But whether or not such mechanisms are operative and important, none of them can immediately or easily be conjoined with standard economic theory in such manner as to take advantage of the insights they may offer.

Concerning the biological-psychological nature of what is here called 'effort', psychologists from at least James and Dewey have made clear that there are physical correlates of effort as consciously experienced. James described effort as follows:

The various degrees of 'effort' actually felt in making the same movement against different resistances are all accounted for by the incoming feelings from our chest, jaws, abdomen, and other parts sympathetically contracted whenever the effort is great.

(James, 1890/1963, p. 368)

Dewey (1897) put it this way:

...I have yet to find a student who, with growing power of introspection, did not report that to him such sensations seemed to constitute the 'feel' of effort. Moreover, the cumulative force of such statements is very great, if not logically conclusive. Many state that if they relax their muscles entirely it is impossible to keep up the effort. Sensations frequently mentioned are those connected with breathing – stopping the respiration, breathing more rapidly, contracted chest and throat; others are contraction of brow, holding head fixed, or twisting it, compression of lips, clenching of fist, contraction of jaws, sensations in pit of stomach, goneness in legs, shoulders higher, head lower than usual, fogginess or mistiness in visual field, trying to see something which eludes vision, etc.

(in McDermott, ed., 1973, pp. 150–1)

Einstein said that at least some of his ideas 'are, in my case, of visual and some of muscular type. Conventional words or other signs have to be sought for laboriously only in a secondary stage...' (Einstein, 1954, p. 26). A variety of evidence to substantiate the point – the sense of effort felt by paraplegics trying to move paralysed limbs is one of the most interesting phenomena – was summarized by Ferrier in 1886 (pp. 383–90).[7]

The physical nature of effort is not of concern here. But it is important to recognize that there are *some* physical correlates, so that it is appropriate to think of effort as exerting some physical 'cost' upon the body. (This does not imply that the sort of cost–benefit analysis that we apply in a variety of business situations is appropriate in thinking about effort; I think it is not helpful, and is likely to twist our thinking in this context.)

Dewey's unusual definition of effort is worth noting:

Practically stated, this means that effort is nothing more, and also nothing less, than tension between means and ends in action, and that the sense of effort is the awareness of this conflict.   (In McDermott, ed., 1973, p.154)

This implies that the greater is the opportunity, or the greater is something like the objective correlates of the Drive–Effort Measure, the greater the effort.

In recent years, psychology has focused on aspects of effort other than the relationship to incentives, and therefore seems to bear little upon the subject discussed here. See Kahneman (1973) for an excellent review of the literature. Also, a good survey of contemporary psychological theorizing about effort, seen from an economist's point of view, is presented by Filer (forthcoming). Much of the psychological discussion involves intervening variables between effort and pay-off, such as expectancy and goal and relative standing (e.g. Locke et al., 1980).

The Viewpoint of this Book

This book aims to increase the power of economic theory to explain *systematically* the amounts and types of work done. The key idea is that the response to a work opportunity depends upon the relationship between the pay-off to the individual's perceived opportunities and his/her present wealth (assuming that Becker's analysis reveals the appropriately specified relationship to be 'positive'). But the measure of motivation is not simply an arithmetic difference between potential and 'endowment', because the same arithmetic gap between the 'before' and 'after' states does not elicit the same change in behaviour in a rich person as in a poor person. (In contrast, in Becker's system the effect of a given change in wealth on the amount of time worked does not depend on wealth position.) Therefore, a function is proposed which makes the difference proportional to the wealth. This function is similar in form to the geometric function often suggested for the curve of diminishing marginal utility of money, and to the shape of the Weber–Fechner psychophysical function.

Involved in an individual's response to an opportunity requiring work are such factors as energy, fatigue, pain, and social constraints which are difficult to model. But because all of these additional factors can be lumped together in the analysis, the net cost in increased size of the theoretical structure is the addition of only one portmanteau variable, to be called Drive–Effort (DrEf for short). And because the intellectual strategy used is to proceed sequentially in two steps – first Becker's analysis as a filter, followed by the Drive–Effort analysis – there are no additional complications in the existing theoretical machinery.

Illustrations of the Nature and Importance
of Variation in Effort

Because the concept of effort is not part of economic theory, the importance of variations in effort is likely to be underestimated by economists. Let us therefore review some observations by business people, journalists, and others which confirm – unless all these first-hand observers are mistaken, or unless the behaviour they refer to is subsumed in some other economic category – that effort really does vary substantially, and that the concept of effort can improve our understanding. Two main types of evidence are, on the one hand, introspection, and, on the other hand, observation of others. There is also some physiological evidence which will be cited first, after which comes evidence concerning DrEf and attention, DrEf and innovation, and then some general observations.

Physiological Evidence for DrEf

Those who have exhorted themselves to 'try harder' physically or mentally in a sporting match or examination, or who have 'racked the brain' in trying to solve a problem, implicitly believe that the outcome does not depend only upon the inputs of time and money. The same is true for circumstances in which you have 'driven' yourself – a telling term – to intensify effort despite unpleasant sensations of pain from fatigue or injury or sickness; also the experience of exerting self-discipline, the essence of which seems to be a capacity to absorb pain for a purpose. We have felt how our capacities to drive ourselves and to exert self-discipline vary with the circumstances, including how much we feel we need the pay-off at risk. We feel how we drive ourselves harder for a crucial point in a sports match, or when we are 'hungry' for victory (another revealing term). Systematic studies of athletics show variation among persons in their willingness to exert this sort of effort:

> Endurance performance . . . is governed by both the physiological capacity of the athlete and the will of the athlete to tolerate pain and the daily sacrifices that are dictated by rigorous training . . . marathoners perform approximately 75 per cent of their

maximal aerobic power with the actual range being from 64–90 per cent of maximum. Maximal aerobic power, or maximal oxygen uptake, is defined by exercise physiologists as the highest oxygen uptake an individual can attain during activity. The decision to perform a level above 75 percent, as opposed to a level below, is certainly a function of will and the ability to cognitively process the cues associated with the pain costs inherent in such a decision. (Silva, 1983, pp. 32–3)

The related phenomenon of mental alertness also has recently been traced to physiological origins:

There is a limit to how mentally alert one can stay. Students burning midnight oil, soldiers on patrol, bankers closing a transatlantic deal all force themselves to work harder and longer than usual, only to collapse in fatigue when the pressure is off. Once they relax, it is difficult to reach such high levels of mental activity again soon. One possible reason is that the brain requires a resting period before it can resume production of the stimulating neuro-transmitters.[8]

DrEf and Attention

Attention, as H. Simon somewhere pointed out, is an important factor of production. The attention of top management often is the bottleneck constraint in an organization, especially where major changes are involved. The amount of attention devoted to a job sometimes is simply a matter of the amount of time that is devoted to a task, as in the case of top management's attention. But sometimes attention depends upon the intensity of effort expended within a fixed work time – for example, where there may be a larger or smaller proportion of daydreaming on the job rather than concentration on the appointed task. Either way, however, it is not easy to increase the amount of needed attention by buying more of it at a constant or declining cost the way a firm can usually buy more building supplies or envelopes. Here are a couple of illustrations:

(1) Limited, Inc. took over the Lane Bryant chain of women's clothing stores:

The task of resuscitating the 207-store chain, catering to

larger and taller women with budget-priced apparel, is occupying 'about 90%' of top management's time, Leslie H. Wexner, chairman and president said in an interview.[9]

(2) One of the advantages claimed for operating a manufacturing operation with very small inventories of input materials which are delivered on a precision schedule (the 'just-in-time' method attributed to the Japanese) is that it draws attention to weak points in the operation:

> The immediate result is work stoppages. Plenty of them. Production comes to a standstill because feeder processes break down or produce too many defectives – and now there is no buffer stock to keep things going. This is exactly what is supposed to happen. For now the analysts and engineers pour out of their offices and mingle with foremen and workers trying to get production going again. Now the causes – bad raw materials, machine breakdown, poor training, tolerances that exceed process capabilities – get attention so that the problem may never recur.[10]

Because attention increases in unit cost as increasing amounts of it are exerted, it has the key property to which the DrEf analysis is addressed.

James makes a great deal of the connection between the concepts of effort and of attention. He writes:

> *Volitional effort is effort of attention . . . The essential achievement of the will, in short, when it is most 'voluntary', is to attend to a difficult object and hold it fast before the mind . . . Effort of attention is thus the essential phenomenon of will . . .* This strain of the attention is the fundamental act of will . . . *Consent to the idea's undivided presence, this is effort's sole achievement.*
>
> (James, 1890/1963, pp. 393–5; italics in original)

James also connects the concepts of effort and attention with decision-making. After a delicate dissection of various kinds of decisions, he describes the final and most deliberative type as follows:

> . . . we feel, in deciding, as if we ourselves by our own wilful act inclined the beam: in the former case by adding our living effort

to the weight of the logical reason which, taken alone, seems powerless to make the act discharge; in the latter by a kind of creative contribution of something instead of a reason which does a reason's work. The slow dead heave of the will that is felt in these instances makes of them a class altogether different subjectively from all the four preceding classes. What the heave of the will betokens metaphysically, what the effort might lead us to infer about a will-power distinct from motives are not matters that concern us yet. Subjectively and phenomenally, the *feeling of effort*, absent from the former decision, accompanies these. Whether it be the dreary resignation for the sake of austere and naked duty of all sorts of rich mundane delights; or whether it be the heavy resolve that of two mutually exclusive trains of future fact, both sweet and good and with no strictly objective or imperative principle of choice between them, one shall forevermore become impossible, while the other shall become reality; it is a desolate and acrid sort of act, an entrance into a lonesome moral wilderness. If examined closely, its chief difference from the former cases appears to be that in those cases the mind at the moment of deciding on the triumphant alternative dropped the other one wholly or nearly out of sight, whereas here both alternatives are steadily held in view, and in the very act of murdering the vanquished possibility the chooser realizes how much in that instant he is making himself lose. It is deliberately driving a thorn into one's flesh; and the sense of *inward effort* with which the act is accompanied is an element which sets this fifth type of decision in strong contrast with the previous four varieties, and makes of it an altogether peculiar sort of mental phenomenon. (James, 1890/1963, pp. 379–80)

DrEf and Innovation

The creation of new ideas that may increase output – that is, the creation of new technology for production and organization – also fits with the DrEf scheme. There would seem to be two major ingredients of idea creation: the urge to attempt creating a new idea, and a range of information that may be synthesized into new knowledge. Discussion of the latter factor will be deferred to another occasion;[11] the former is of interest here.

Ever since at least Hicks (1932/1963, pp. 125–7), economists have distinguished between autonomous and induced inventions. It is quite clear, as Schmookler (1966) especially has shown,[12] that the extent of the economic opportunity (the amount of investment, in Schmookler's empirical work; change in relative prices, in Hicks's theorizing) induces some inventions, and hence it seems reasonable to liken that factor to the extent of Drive. And autonomous inventions also are likely to depend on some urge to astonish the scientific world, or to advance one's career, or to improve mankind's lot, rather than being the result simply of curiosity uninfluenced by economic or psychological needs. Hence it probably is reasonable to include autonomous inventions in the discussion, though there is no necessity to do so here.

Change of any kind, including adjustment of one's ideas and institutions, requires effort. As Veblen (1890/1953, p. 137) put it, 'All change in habits of life and thought is irksome', and 'any innovation calls for a greater expenditure of nervous energy in making the necessary readjustment than would otherwise be the case' (p. 140). Veblen well described how wealth reduces the propensity to make such adjustments:

> If any portion or class of society is sheltered from the action of the environment in any essential respect, that portion of the community, or that class, will adapt its views and its scheme of life more tardily to the altered general situation; it will in so far tend to retard the process of social transformation. The wealthy leisure class is in such a sheltered position with respect to the economic forces that make for change and readjustment. And it may be said that the forces which make for a readjustment of institutions, especially in the case of a modern industrial community, are, in the last analysis, almost entirely of an economic nature. (p. 134)
>
> The members of the wealthy class do not yield to the demand for innovation as readily as other men because they are not constrained to do so. (p. 138)

General Introspective Evidence

Consider these extracts from an article headed 'Some Japanese Balk at Overseas Jobs':

The trend [of Japanese executives refusing overseas assignments] seems to symbolize . . . the 'diminishing fighting spirit' of Japanese businessmen, particularly younger businessmen. Unlike their seniors, who put loyalty to the company above all else, many of these younger men seem to care most about their family lives and other personal concerns, it is said. One personnel chief says establishing the loyalty of younger employees is the crucial challenge for Japanese companies in the 1980's.[13]

Another example comes from interviews with young Japanese executives studying at Stanford:

American training may help Mr. Abe and his fellows to manage an increasingly leisure-minded Japanese work force. Says a Japanese classmate of Mr. Abe's: 'We still feel we belong to the company, but that is lessening. Young people in Japan now like to leave the office at 5 o'clock. American management has been dealing with worker independence for a long time, and being here will help us deal with it when we return.'[14]

It would seem plausible that the trend of increasing well-offness with passing years explains an important part of the Japanese executives' behaviour.

This passage comes from Cahan's famous novel-from-the-life, *The Rise of David Levinsky*:

There are moments when I am overwhelmed by a sense of my success and ease . . . I recalled other people whom I used to fear and before whom I used to humiliate myself because of my poverty. I thought of the time when I had already entered the cloak business, but was struggling and squirming and constantly racking my brains for some way of raising a hundred dollars; when I would cringe with a certain East Side banker and vainly beg him to extend a small note of mine, and come away in a sickening state of despair.

(Quoted by Rischin, 1965, pp. 209–10)

Here is testimony by a football player about himself and colleagues on one of the most successful professional teams of all time: '[S]o many of us were living proof that deprivation was a great motivator.'[15]

General Observational Evidence

With respect to other persons' behaviour, we not only observe that effort varies with the circumstances, but as consumers and employers we also act upon that observation. We offer extra pay to a taxi driver to 'try' to make the airport in time for the plane. We give bonuses for superior performance in business and in professional athletics. Sellers will literally pay prospective buyers to 'try' new products.[16] People demand extra compensation to do work which may besmirch their reputations, such as crossing a picket line; the other side of the same coin is that people will pay to receive 'honours' such as titles of nobility, or the opportunity to perform some religious ritual (the auction of the high-prestige roles in the Torah-reading ceremony in orthodox synagogues on Jewish high holidays used to be a fascinating drama of pride and charity). Purchase of honours is consistent with Adam Smith's assertion that our reputation in the community is the good which is of most importance to most of us.

The premium paid for effort is not very different from the premium paid for bodily risk. This is seen when the taxi driver racing to the airport not only suffers the stress of trying but also braves the danger of a painful crash. The same must be true of a Sherpa porter carrying baggage in a difficult and dangerous Nepalese mountain ascent. (Such danger to life and limb surely goes beyond the risk to one's human capital and future stream of income.)

The exertion of effort, with its concomitant elements of pain, fatigue, ego, and pride is one of the biggest differences between the robot and the human as factors of production. Both require energy to operate. Work time is a variable to both. Both can be programmed to check their physical conditions and to make repairs if indicated. But a robot has no ego, and it does not suffer mental or physical pain.[17] (Of course, one might translate pain into a physical deterioration, but this would blur our understanding rather than contribute to it.)

Here are some comments on the effect of hard times in increasing firms' effort in cost-cutting and marketing.

The president of United Airlines:

In difficult economic circumstances such as we have experienced in the past few years, there is a temptation to sacrifice quality to reduce costs or increase profits ... American businesspeople, lulled into complacency by an extended period of dominance in world markets, have allowed quality to deteriorate in a misguided effort to catch up when they realized our nation had fallen behind. (Ferris, 1982)

About the 'smokestack industries' in recent recessions:

Pessimists who have been lamenting the passing of the nation's basic industry were premature. The economic recovery is starting to show up in big profits for smokestack plants . . . painful cut-backs have lowered heavy industry's break-even point . . . and are a major reason for the return to acceptable profits.

'Everything is lean and mean about this company except its chairman', says Richard J. Jacob, the bulky chairman and chief executive officer of Dayco Corp.[18]

From a German executive of a company that had been close to bankruptcy: 'The struggle for survival triggers many energies.'[19]

A poll on the subject in a *Wall Street Journal* article was entitled 'Executives See Some Benefits In Recession':

Now that it's over, business executives don't have such bad things to say about the recession.

'We had sloppy habits that had to change', says the chairman of an oil company. Says the chairman of a manufacturing company: 'It put a dose of reality into our lives – sharpened us up. It was an educational tool.' Adds the president of a retailing concern: 'It got economic sense into us.'

These are among the findings of a *Wall Street Journal*/Gallup survey of 822 executives. The survey shows that more than seven in 10 top executives at large and medium-sized companies think the recession was a good thing for the country. Only about two in 10 thought it was a bad thing . . .

Here is a sampling of what executives had to say about whether the slump was good or bad:

'People are more realistic. Workers are more realistic about the value and quality of their labor and the value of competition. It woke business executives up to realize their irresponsible wage and labor practices. In short, everyone was scared to death.'

the chairman of a large company

'It was a well-justified adjustment. We were wasting money
. . . It still isn't corrected totally, but it has improved.'

the chairman of a real estate company

'Hardship on people is not a good thing. Perhaps it was
medicine we need, although I hate to say it.'

the chairman of a company that recycles scrap metal

'We were all at a point in this country where everyone was
satisfied, businessmen in particular. We had gotten to the point
where we weren't concentrating on things as we should, and this
helped bring us back to reality.'

the president of a petroleum-shipping company

'It made us bite the bullet and realize what Japan is doing.'

the president of an advertising company

'It weeded out a lot of fat in the industrial complex, but it's
unfortunate that it had to happen.'

the president of a coal company

'From a cold-blooded economic stand-point it was good, but
what a human tragedy.'

the president of a petroleum jobber

'It put us all in our place. Taught us the value of a dollar and
made us appreciate what we've got. Also, it made us realize that
it could be a hell of a lot worse. I never heard of anyone go
without a meal.'

the president of a paint and wallpaper store[20]

A journalist's observation about the effect on AT&T of operating
with competition:

New York – Part of American Telephone & Telegraph Co.'s
effort to reach out in new directions is an intensifying program
to trim a work force that in the old days was as stable and secure
as AT&T's own profits and dividends.

The old stability ended with the breakup of AT&T on Jan. 1,
which plunged the company into a fast-track battle for computer
and tele-communications markets in this country and worldwide. In this race, AT&T quickly found it could not carry its

old overhead and employee costs, its officials say. 'It's a difficult adjustment, but it is very much a part of the competitive world we're entering', said Francis J. Heffron, executive vice president for planning and administration at AT&T Technologies . . . It is a painful process.[21]

And the drop in oil prices:

Big U.S. oil companies, once fat and happy, have been eliminating jobs by the tens of thousands, and white-collar employees have been hit hardest.

One reason why Exxon Corp.'s earnings rose a healthy 19 per cent last year was that the company eliminated 17,000 positions in 1983 – 10% of its entire worldwide work force. It cut another 7,000 jobs in 1982. 'We needed to go on a diet and exercise program', says George B. McCullough, Exxon's vice president for employee relations. 'We needed to get down to fighting trim?

Most big oil companies, faced with keener competition because of sagging prices and demand, are thinking the same way . . .

'We were fat in a lot of areas', says a Sun spokesman. When you have some very, very prosperous years, you're sometimes not as careful as you should be.'[22]

Foreign competition caused General Motors to examine all parts of its operation to cut cost:

At 'Scrub U.', GM's Janitors Learn Latest Ways to Get the Dirt Out . . .

Even the mundane can't escape the visionary gaze of General Motors Corp. management these days. And it is hard to get much more mundane than mopping floors.

In fact, just as GM's new Saturn Corp. is meant to revolutionize car-building, the company's new Industrial Cleaning Technology Center here is meant to turn the world of cleaning commercial dirt and grime upside down. If cleanliness is next to godliness, then 'Scrub U.' – as it is known throughout GM – is almost heaven . . . 'To regain competitiveness we have to attack absolutely every area of the business that generates cost', says Robert J. Eaton, vice president of advanced product and manufacturing activities.[23]

Even some economists use the vocabulary of effort:

Edward Denison of the Brookings Institution . . . says 'the fear of Japanese competition' is driving both management and labor to look harder for cost-saving efficiencies.

and

'We are seeing cost-cutting in the business world the likes of which hasn't taken place since the 1930's', says A. Gary Shilling, a New York consultant. Because of the expectations of slow economic growth, weak exports and foreign competition, he adds, 'cost-cutting is going to be one of the motifs of business for the rest of this decade. And cost-cutting has as its counterpoint unemployment for somebody.'[24]

A student of the economics of research and development uses an effort concept in describing the effects of government intervention:

Why face the uncertainties of a new technology and the inconveniences of change if the State stands ready to guarantee markets, or to make up deficits incurred in trying to hold a position with inappropriate products or methods? (Carter, 1983)

Managers as well as industrial psychologists believe that a worker's effort is influenced by his or her 'motivation'. We read accounts of the effect of the recession of the early 1980s about the auto industry:

Unions Say Auto Firms Use Interplant Rivalry To Raise Work Quotas . . . Locals Call It 'Whipsawing', Complain That It Works Because of Layoff Fears.[25]

And this one about a truck parts firm:

Like many other companies, Eaton has also increased its emphasis on employee motivation. 'We assume that people want to make a contribution and that we have to create an atmosphere to permit them to make the contribution', says Mr. Stover. 'That includes everything from eating and parking facilities to first-line supervisor relationships.'[26]

And this about a tyre maker:

Firestone is putting new emphasis on employee motivation. 'We were no better and no worse than other companies', says John J. Nevin, Firestone's chief executive, 'but only about 1,000 of our employees were permitted to contribute everything they could. Tacitly, we said to the rest, "We're not buying your brains; we're buying your body"'. Now, Firestone is trying to harness that 'underutilized asset – the brainpower of its employees', Mr. Nevin says, through a wide-ranging program to involve them in cutting costs and improving product quality.[27]

One of the most difficult choices that every society, other than the most brutal of them, must make is the trade-off between what we may dub 'character' (or discipline) and 'compassion' (or caring, or pity). All but the most blindly devoted mothers and fathers recognize that giving people economic resources instead of requiring that they obtain them through work may reduce the propensity for work. This idea is at the core of Murray's recent *Losing Ground* (1984). Or consider this statement of the effects of want on a young Hispanic American:

... my only out was to promise myself that these hands were never going to harvest tomatoes, not for anybody. White people can go to hell in a handbasket – they can go to Burger King and *not* have it their way, for all I care – I was not going to harvest lettuce. That somehow, I was going to make it.[28]

Abraham Lincoln wrote to his brother in 1851:

Your request for eighty dollars I do not think it best to comply with now. At the various times when I have helped you a little you have said to me, 'We can get along very well now'; but in a very short time I find you in the same difficulty again. Now, this can only happen by some defect in your conduct. What that defect is, I think I know. You are not lazy, and still you are an idler. I doubt whether, since I saw you, you have done a good whole day's work in any one day. You do not very much dislike to work, and still you do not work much, merely because it does not seem to you that you could get much out of it. This habit of uselessly wasting time is the whole difficulty; it is vastly important to you, and still more so to your children, that you should break the habit. It is more important to them, because they have longer to live, and can keep out of an idle habit before

they are in it, easier than they can get out after they are in.
(Tarbell, 1911, p. 13, as quoted somewhere by Novak)

And Mandeville wrote acerbically that:

Pity [by which he means the urging of compassionate acts
without regard to their full consequences], though it is the most
gentle and the least mischievous of all our passions, is yet as
much a frailty of our nature as anger, pride, or fear. The weakest
minds have generally the greatest share of it, for which reason
none are more compassionate than women and children. It must
be owned that of all our weaknesses, it is the most amiable and
bears the greatest resemblance to virtue; nay, without a
considerable mixture of it, the society could hardly subsist: but
as it is an impulse of nature that consults neither the public
interest nor our own reason, it may produce evil as well as good.
It has helped to destroy the honour of virgins and corrupted the
integrity of judges; and whoever acts from it as a principle, what
good soever he may bring to the society, has nothing to boast of,
but that he has indulged a passion that has happened to be
beneficial to the public.   (Mandeville, 1705/1962, pp. 49–50)

I hope that you the reader are by now sufficiently convinced of the
importance of the effort concept in understanding economic action
that you will proceed to the formal statement of it in the next two
chapters.

Notes

1   The validity of the Hawthorne conclusion has been the subject of hot
controversy in the recent sociology literature (Carey, 1967; Franke and
Kaul, 1978; Schlaifer, 1980; Franke, 1980; and also the important early
treatment by Viteles, 1932).
2   The dynamic effects of exerting effort are an important topic in
themselves; they are not treated in this book but deserve future
attention.
3   I hope it is not reaching too far afield to offer the following quotation
from Berlin:
     . . . because the life which Churchill so loves presents itself to him
     in a historical guise as part of the pageant of tradition, his method
     of constructing historical narrative, the distribution of emphasis,

the assignment of relative importance to persons and events, the theory of history, the architecture of the narrative, the structure of the sentences, the words themselves, are elements in an historical revival as fresh, as original, and as idiosyncratic as the neoclassicism of the Renaissance or the Regency. To complain that this omits altogether too much by assuming that the impersonal, the dull, the undramatic, are necessarily also unimportant, may well be just; but to lament that this is not contemporary, and therefore in some way less true, less responsive to modern needs, than the noncommittal, neutral grass and plastic of those objective historians who regard facts and only facts as interesting and, worse still, all facts as equally interesting – what is this but craven pedantry and blindness?

4 *New York Times*, 31 October 1982, p. 24F. The possibility of misquotation must always be considered, and hence this should be taken as exemplary rather than as a commentary on Samuelson.

5 Haim Levy informed me that this is the current state of knowledge in the finance literature.

6 I do not doubt that the exertion of effort often is preferred to no exertion, as seen in many unpaid activities such as sports, and in the activities of young children and pet dogs. But I do not think that this affects the analysis offered here, for the purposes to which it is directed.

7 I am grateful to Jay Russo for sending me this source.

8 *Newsweek*, 7 February 1983, p. 46.

9 *Wall Street Journal*, 12 October 1982, p. 24.

10 *Wall Street Journal*, 15 November 1982, editorial page.

11 A single note on this topic: a faster rate of change in the environment over the individual's lifetime is likely to produce a wider range of informational stimuli. And migration – which constitutes a change of environments by the individual – also is likely to increase the range of such informational stimuli.

12 See also: Scherer, 1982.

13 *Wall Street Journal*, 9 July 1982, p. 14.

14 *Wall Street Journal*, 20 October 1982, p. 16.

15 Jerry Kramer, quoted by Jonathan Yardley in *Washington Post*, 23 October 1985, p. C2, from *Distant Replay* (New York Putnam, 1985).

16 Seen in the newspaper ten minutes after this sentence was written: SYNERGY DEPT.: In East Palestine, Ohio, a dental clinic and a Ford dealership team up to promote themselves. A dental chair will be put in the auto showroom. Persons who test-drive a car will get their teeth cleaned free. (*Wall Street Journal*, 26 August, 1982, p. 1)

17 Robots could fire people for non-performance, or foreclose mortgages for non-payment, but would not agonize over the decision the way a person does. This vignette about rural bankers refusing rollover loans to overextended farmers brings out the point:

> The financial logic may be clear, but bankers say such decisions aren't easily made. Refusing a loan may mean ending what has been a way of life for generations. In others, it means cutting loose young men who have little hope of finding work in a weak economy. The process is especially painful for rural bankers in close-knit farm communities. 'These guys sit next to you in church', says Bryant Wackman, a bank president in Brooklyn, Wis., who may have to decline loans for two of his customers. 'You've cooked all those chicken barbecues, eaten the smoke with them for years. It's difficult.'
> (*Wall Street Journal*, 21 December 1982, p. 21)

Hofstadter observes that under appropriate circumstances humans will always get bored and frustrated but computers do not (unless programmed to do so). This leads humans to think about the task (that is to move up a hierarchical level of thinking), which is a crucial characteristic of human thinking, in his view:

> [I]t is possible for a machine to act unobservant; it is impossible for a human to act unobservant . . . if somebody says that some task is 'mechanical', it does not mean that people are incapable of doing the task; it implies, though, that only a machine could do it over and over without ever complaining, or feeling bored.
> (Hofstadter, 1979, p. 37)

18 'Streamlined Smokestack Industries Are Beginning to Show Big Profits', *Wall Street Journal*, 28 March 1984, p. 35.

19 Detlev Rohwedder, 'A Panel of European Business Executives Sees Narrowing of Gap with U.S., Japan', *Wall Street Journal*, 26 June 1985, p. 30.

20 *Wall Street Journal*, 13 January 1984, p. 25.

21 'The Painful Downsizing of AT&T', *Washington Post*, 2 September 1984, p. G1.

22 'Major Oil Firms Are Slashing Jobs As Takeovers Rise, Demand Sags', *Wall Street Journal*, 19 April 1984, p. 33.

23 *Wall Street Journal*, 21 May 1985, p. 33.

24 *Wall Street Journal*, 9 May 1983, p. 1.

25 *Wall Street Journal*, 7 November 1983, p. 1.

26 *Wall Street Journal*, 28 March 1984, p. 35.

27 *Wall Street Journal*, 11 May 1983, p. 22.

28 'Where Anglos Fear to Tread', *Washington Post*, 6 March 1984, p. C11.

3

Theoretical Context

What is Needed

The theory necessary to understand the behaviour of firms can be simpler than the theory necessary to understand the behaviour of individuals. For example, when discussing the firm, it is usually reasonable to assume that the firm maximizes the real present value of the stream of future money incomes and expenditures. For some analytic purposes it may be necessary also to consider the risk of various alternatives, or the effect on stock prices. But it will seldom be necessary to consider ethical and social constraints such as the desire for community good will. And when such a constraint must be considered, it often may be treated with an eye to the present value of the firm rather than as an end in itself; this enables the objective function to be simple. Furthermore, one does not need to consider the number of hours the firm works in total or on average. Nor does one need to consider the effort the firm makes in one activity or another, apart from consideration of all the real resources expended, unless some efforts made by individual employees affect them or their fellows negatively or positively in such a manner as to affect the future smooth working of the organization.

If one wishes to understand the economic behaviour of individuals or of non-profit groups, however, the objective function often cannot be assumed to be so simple. Here a distinction is necessary: when economists discuss a firm, their interest invariably is in the firm's economic behaviour. But some economists' interest in individuals and groups – for example, Becker's interest in household behaviour, and Schelling's (1960) and Boulding's (1977) interest in conflict – is in understanding behaviour for reasons that go beyond its economic effects, that is, for more general scientific reasons. In contrast, as noted earlier, the interest of this book is only in the acts of individuals and groups that affect the economic (or purchasing power) status of themselves and of others. This makes possible the omission of some elements that are necessary in the more general enquiry into human behaviour that interests theorists of household and conflict behaviour. On the other hand the subject of this book may require bringing into the analysis such elements as creativity and self-discipline that may reasonably be omitted from economic approaches to the study of human behaviour for its own sake.

The Nature of the Question

The general question being addressed here is: Will an individual or a group such as a nation, undertake a particular economic opportunity which involves increased work effort?[1] There are two types of sub-questions: (a) Will an alternative that would increase total money income – such as working more intensively, or spending extra time weeding the family farm plot, or reopening the store door to serve a customer after customary closing time, or pushing back the closing time itself – be undertaken or rejected? Will an independent mason accept a small contract to fix a driveway, or a mathematics tutor take on another student, or a factory worker accept proffered overtime work this evening? And (b) Will an alternative that seems not to be 'profitable' in money terms – such as building the world's highest cathedral in the Middle Ages, or contributing one's time to distributing food to the starving – be undertaken anyway? Questions of both types may both be considered as inquiries into the extent to which people act like the *homo economicus* in the popular caricature. But the aim here is not to throw light on that ideal type, but rather to understand the output of economic goods by various individuals and nations at various times.

A firm's decision problem may be characterized as choosing those among the available set of alternatives which will produce maximum profit from its given stock of resources (including its line of credit);

this stock of resources can be specified in advance of the decision. There is no benefit to the firm from leaving some resources unused, except perhaps the opportunity to perform maintenance work on its capital equipment, which can be reckoned objectively along with everything else in the calculation. The firm's decision process can be seen as first constructing a ladder of alternatives, and then selecting that subset of the best alternatives which together will yield maximum profit, using whichever technical criterion of profit may be appropriate.

Not all of the resources available to an individual can be specified in the same fashion as for a firm, however. And therefore the individual's decision about a work opportunity is not perfectly analogous to that of the firm.

The individual's opportunity-accepting decision may be modelled as a business-like decision subject to additional constraints – first, the constraint of the reservation price for additional work time, as determined systematically by the sort of time-allocation process among production and consumption activities that Becker analysed (1965); and secondly, the set of constraints related to the individual's own physical and mental attributes. The latter constraints may be thought of as analogous to the variety of needs and tastes that influence purchasing decisions for consumption. All of these latter constraints can, I believe, be fruitfully dealt with as a single variable, the Drive–Effort factor (DrEf).

The Theoretical Framework Offered Here

For convenience, let us deal with simple decisions in which all consequences, except for the carrying-over of profit from period to period, occur within a single short period. That is, no long-lived capital equipment needs to be purchased, and no long-run contracts or customer relationships are involved, in the examples to be discussed. In such cases, the individual begins by comparing expected income (money revenue) with outgo (expenditures on purchased inputs). If the income does not exceed the outgo, the opportunity need not be considered further unless there are other benefits to be considered, for example, charitable benefits, the consideration of which may be deferred until later. That is, if total revenue R exceeds total expenditure C, excluding the value of the decision-maker's time, the alternative will be considered further; if not, not. This calculation of the lower boundary of 'gross profit' is the first step in the sequential decision-making process (one which is not mentioned by Becker, though, perhaps because it seems too obvious).

Clearly, however, many alternatives where $R > C$ in money are not undertaken; the individual is limited by, if nothing else, having only 24 hours in the day. Economists have long used the notion of a 'reservation price' (Davenport, 1913/1968, p. 128) to explain why some alternatives with $R > C$ are not accepted. But the matter was not understood systematically until Becker's 1965 work, where he showed how to compute the reservation price as a function of the individual's income, wealth, time intensity of consumption possibilities, and time budget.

Becker's Analysis Compared to This One

Our present interest in Becker's analysis is how a change in a person's wealth affects the amount of time spent working. The answer may be read from Becker's equation (and using his notation):

$$\Sigma(p_i b_i + t_i \bar{w}) Z_i = V + T_w \tag{3.1}$$

where

p_i = unit price of market good i

b_i = amount of given market good i necessary to produce a unit of Z_i

t_i = input of time necessary to produce a unit of Z_i, in combination with b_i

$\bar{w}$ = average wage per hour worked, assumed constant

Z_i = a commodity that enters the person's utility function

V = 'wealth endowment', the person's assets for spending in the current period

T = time endowment = 24 hours per day

T_i = time spent in consuming the ith commodity = $t_i Z_i$

T_c = time spent in consumption = $\sum_{i}^{m} T_i = T - T_w$

T_w = time spent working

If we assume (as Becker does in his main analysis) that there are constant returns in producing Z_i so that b_i and t_i are fixed for the given w and the prevailing p_i, and if the Z_i are those that are consumed in equilibrium, then

$$\frac{dZ_i}{dV} = \text{constant} > 0 \tag{3.2}$$

Therefore

$$\frac{dT_i}{dV} > 0 \tag{3.3}$$

And

$$\frac{dT_c}{dV} > 0 \tag{3.4}$$

That is, total time spent on consumption increases with an increase in wealth, which is commonsensical for most situations. And since the time spent on work, $T_w = T - T_c$, then

$$\frac{dT_w}{dV} < 0 \tag{3.5}$$

That is, the amount of time spent working varies inversely with wealth, holding wages constant.

This conclusion may also be found in Becker's expanded life-cycle framework (1976). The effect of wealth upon saving, a related issue from the standpoint of economic development, may also be seen clearly in the same framework. That expanded life-cycle framework also has clear implications for such phenomena as the effect of a change in life expectancy upon work and saving.

Becker's system, however, was not framed to comprehend the sort of economic opportunity of main interest here.[2] His formal analysis deals with a situation in which the wage is constant, that is, where the marginal earnings per hour equal the average earnings. Becker (1976, p. 93) also mentions the situation in which 'marginal wage-rates were below average ones', but he notes that in such case the key 'resource constraint in [his relevant] equation would not have any particularly useful interpretation'; the situation of a farmer for whom there are diminishing returns to weeding illustrates this case.

The most interesting economic opportunities, however, are those that have expected pay-offs per hour *higher* than average pay-offs to presently-undertaken opportunities. They are particularly interesting because they are unusually valuable (by their very definition) from a private as well as social point of view. They also are likely to be particularly valuable socially in the long run because they represent change, that is, a break with preceding activity.

There are two ways an individual or a nation can respond to a new high-pay-off opportunity. One way is to rearrange one's entire set of work opportunities so that the high-pay-off opportunity would have priority ahead of some existing opportunities which are presently accepted; in that case, some presently-marginal opportunities would probably be bumped out of the presently-accepted set. This process would be roughly equivalent to a wage increase, and the overall amount of work might go up or down, as discussed by the traditional theory as well as by Becker. This response could be analysed formally, but the complicated nature of the rise in 'wage' would make the analysis complex, and in any case, such analysis is not necessary here.

The new opportunity also could be responded to as an *additional* opportunity, while continuing to fulfill the previously-decided-upon work schedule. In this case, if the new opportunity can be accepted in greater or smaller amounts, rather than just yes-or-no, Becker's analysis implies that at least *some* amount of the additional opportunity would be accepted. This can be seen directly from the following reasoning: assume that the present set of work decisions implies that the value of the marginal unit of time spent in consumption equals the value of the marginal unit of time spent in production. If the latter value increases, on most assumptions the work-time decision must change (work must increase) as a new point of equality of the marginal quantities is determined.

These two ways of looking at the matter correspond to different responses over the life cycle of an opportunity. When the opportunity first appears, and before there is time to rearrange commitments, the opportunity must be dealt with as if all else is fixed and the new one must be an addition. But with the passage of time, commitments loosen and the new opportunity can be dealt with as its priority would suggest. Without further analysis, it can be seen that a rich new opportunity would *eventually* lead to less work, *ceteris paribus*, by making the person wealthier (by way of increasing the income from the now-fixed-into-the-schedule better opportunities, which can now be seen as an 'endowment' or 'wealth' in Becker's analysis).

But even expanded, Becker's framework would not complete the story. This is clearly seen when we notice that some alternatives which pass the Becker time test are not undertaken. To repeat, examples include (a) work which is unethical or unpleasant or dangerous to the reputation; and (b) work which requires leaving one's family and friends. These examples undoubtedly could be squeezed into the Becker framework by supplying some shadow prices, but this would be so tortuous that it would do serious violence to the time-allocation analysis.

A more recent paper by Becker (1983), circulated after the first draft of this book was completed, expands his framework and includes a concept of effort that helps to delineate the difference between the context of his interest and the context of this book. Becker equates effort with the expenditure of energy, whereas I equate it with a much wider range of personal goods such as reputation, and with accepting pain, as well as with the use of human energy. Becker's definition enables him to assume plausibly that the total supply of effort by a person is fixed over the period of analysis, which may be a reasonable assumption for some applications of his theory. But the essence of the analysis offered here is that it applies to contexts in which the total effort is variable rather than fixed.

The difference between Becker's approach and mine does not hinge on different biological assumptions. It may be that the supply of effort over an entire lifetime is indeed fixed, either at birth or later on, in which case more effort being exerted this year implies less capacity for effort next year, or else it implies a shorter lifespan within which to exert effort; such may or may not be the case, but either way it has no implication for the analysis given here (though if it is grossly not the case, it might complicate Becker's analysis).[3] Rather, the analysis offered here is intended to fit a case in which the focus is upon a particular period within which a person may or may not change total effort – a given month or year or decade – whereas Becker mainly focuses on *allocation* of some total within a conservation-of-energy framework.

In the present framework there may also be an increase in effort expended in work at the expense of effort expended in consuming, as in Becker's analysis, but that case serves to bring out the difference between Becker's and this analysis even more sharply. An increase in economic opportunity in Becker's framework – typically an increase in the wage rate – may lead to greater *or* less expenditure of total effort in work, because capacity to enjoy non-working time by buying more commodities is increased by the wage increase; this is exactly analogous to the possibility of a backward-bending supply curve of work time. But such a possibility does not exist within the framework offered here because the new opportunity is considered as being separate from the old opportunity set, and in the 'temporary' period under analysis the new opportunity does not replace the old opportunity set. To illustrate: imagine that to induce you to work shovelling manure for the next hour instead of sitting at your desk, a person offers you a sum three times as great as you have ever earned for an hour's work. There is no way that the offer can decrease your effort during the next hour (apart from unusual psychological twists not under consideration here) and it may increase it; such is the subject of the analysis offered here. Becker's analysis suggests that the manure-shovelling offer may decrease the total effort for the day or lifetime beginning with this hour, and that might well be the case. But in the framework offered here, the decision for the subsequent hours is assumed to be made separately of the decision for this hour, and will use different data, to wit, the increased wealth (or 'property income', in Becker's framework) at the start of the next period (compared to the wealth if the manure-shovelling opportunity is not offered or accepted), which may reduce effort later on. And this subsequent reduction in effort is also an important part of the analysis offered here, and is part and parcel of many of the applications. But that subsequent reduction is not part of an allocation process; rather, it is the result of an allocation having been made separately.

The point of contact between Becker's and this analysis – the point at which they are consistent – is the effect of 'property income' or 'wealth'; an increase leads to reduction in work effort. And this point of contact helps highlight the difference in the approaches: Becker implicitly envisions an increase in wage opportunity as extending over a lifetime, within which long period it has an effect like an increase in property income, along with its main effect, leaving the overall impact ambiguous. My analysis envisions the new opportunity as applying to the present short period apart from later periods (even if it will extend to a lifetime), and the resulting increase in wealth at the end of this present period is analysed separately as such; hence both effects – within this period and within the next – are determinate.

The increase in amount of time worked when a market opens up to hitherto-subsistence farmers illustrates the difference between Becker's theory and the Drive–Effort hypothesis: a market opens up trade opportunities where there were none, and therefore increases the Drive–Effort Measure. It would be hard to deduce this result from Becker's theory. One could view this phenomenon simply as an increase in 'wages', but it would hardly be simply an increase in a constant wage level, which makes difficult a deduction from Becker's time theory.

General Statement of the Drive–Effort Concept

Earlier it was noted that many elements other than money and time cost may influence a person not to undertake a job or project. Consider these examples as representative: (a) the fatigue and/or pain which accompanies physical and mental effort; (b) the loss of reputation and the incurring of social disapproval for undertaking work which is against social customs (for example, breaking a strike, or working with a lower caste); and (c) the fear of loss which accompanies the risk of an uncertain enterprise. Not all the factors opposing work operate in any given situation, of course. But it is reasonable to think that all of them are monotonic, and to the extent that they operate, all increase in force with the amount of time spent working at a task. If so, we can treat them all as a single negative factor – a 'cost' – incurred when a person works.

Let us label 'Drive' (denoted 'Dr') the tendency to respond with work to a particular set of conditions, and 'Effort' (denoted 'Ef') the force which a person exerts in order to overcome the congeries of work-resisting forces.[4] Drive is equivalent in magnitude to the amount of effort a person *would be willing* to expend in response to a given set of conditions.

When discussing the motivation of an individual or group, Dr and Ef may be thought of as the joint concept Drive–Effort (DrEf), the objective work effort that one is willing to expend in a given situation in response to the subjective driving impulse. In some contexts it may be appropriate to speak of Dr and Ef separately, while in other contexts it is appropriate to talk of DrEf as a single concept.

Throughout this book, the effort that one *would* expend must be distinguished from the work effort that one *must* expend in order actually to undertake a given opportunity. These concepts will be specified more precisely in the formal analysis of monopoly and duopoly in chapter 6.

The Drive–Effort Measure may be viewed as a synonym for 'incentive'. Economists frequently use the term 'incentive', and in fact, many regard it as a fundamental concept of economic analysis. But in current economic writing, incentive is an ambiguous concept. It may be intended as objective – the price or expected pay-off for an activity. Or it may be thought of as subjective, as in a phrase like 'That pay-off will not be an incentive to her.' The approach suggested here should be helpful in separating these two meanings, Drive–Effort standing for the private subjective meaning of incentive (which can, however, be measured objectively by the scientist, if so desired), and price or expected pay-off representing the public meaning. Hopefully, this essay makes a contribution by rendering the incentive concept more precise, and then showing how application of the concept as defined rigorously can lead to a variety of useful conclusions.

The actual work effort required by, or done in response to, a particular opportunity may be less than the potential Ef, of course. Drive–Effort plus time plus money wealth may be thought of as 'full wealth', following Becker's usage. That is, we may think of three inputs into a revenue-producing alternative: money expenditures, time, and work effort. (Reputation and other dimensions might also be added.) An alternative conceptual approach, which is not followed up here but which some might find helpful, is to think of effort as a dimension of 'effective' work time just as the skill of the person deriving from the person's human capital is an element of 'effective' work time.

Sociologists and psychologists will point out that, for humans, the mental states or properties commonly called values and attitudes are part of the causal nexus involving Drive–Effort. The model that underlies the treatment of these matters in this paper is as in figure 3.1.[5]

In question is the promptness with which values and attitudes respond to changes in economic circumstances; if they were to

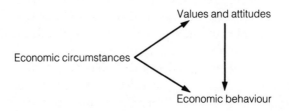

Figure 3.1 The place of values and attitudes in the theoretical context

respond instantly, we would not need to consider them as having an independent existence in this context. An example (taken from Freedman, 1961–2) is attitudes toward, and values about, having children. The views commonly referred to as Jewish, Islamic, and Catholic religious thinking surely have affected (and still affect) the number of children born in poor countries with high child mortality. But families originating in those high-fertility communities come to have much lower fertility when they move to economically advanced countries, despite continuing the same religious affiliations. (For example, in the United States, fertility of Catholics is now nearly the same as fertility of Protestants.) The shift in fertility does not take place immediately upon immigration, but rather requires at least the good part of a generation. So it seems that values and attitudes markedly affect fertility behaviour in the shorter run, but less so or not at all in the longer run. This suggests that values and attitudes themselves change under the pressure of economic circumstances. By the same reasoning, it would be reasonable to expect a lagged change in DrEf and in observed work effort after wealth has changed.

Perhaps a word about other intermediate-state concepts would be helpful here. Speaking in the vernacular, a *ceteris paribus* reduction in a person's wealth makes a person more 'hungry' and increases the person's 'needs'. I assume that this will increase a person's 'drive', the latter being a psychological concept, though psychologists may postulate some circumstances in which a reduction in wealth may reduce rather than increase drive, e.g. by discouraging a person. The increased drive would seem to be experienced as greater 'desire' for the pay-off from a given opportunity, and perhaps leads to higher goals being set, because the person 'needs' more. On the other hand, a psychologist might postulate that in some circumstances an increase in need (using the word 'need' loosely now, and to be distinguished from the psychological concept of 'need for . . .') may cause a lowering of aspirations and goals, and hence perhaps less drive, because of a complex of other psychological mechanisms. But for the purposes of economic analysis it seems useful to assume a monotonic function of the sort embodied in the Drive–Effort Measure. And a monotonic formulation has the advantage that it can be tested empirically; a non-monotonic function cannot be tested so easily.

With respect to opportunity, the psychologist may wish to view the relationship as including expectancy of gain, and perception of the probability of success or failure, as intermediate variables. And opportunity may alter the structure of wants and values in complex ways. There seems nothing in such more complex theorizing about the psychological mechanisms that runs counter to the Drive–Effort hypothesis, however.

As noted earlier, unlike the situation with respect to time, it does not seem sensible to attribute to a person a fixed amount of available Drive–Effort; there does not seem to be a reasonable way to measure DrEf as a proportion of a fixed quantity. For example, DrEf trades off with sleep; additional sleep increases one's capacity to endure pain, but reduces the amount of time available for work. That is, acknowledging the composite of factors involved in DrEf complicates the notion of a fixed quantity of time available to the person for work and the consumption of goods (assuming sleep is not a consumption good). The intellectual problem, then, is to model DrEf with respect to the conditions which affect its strength in a given individual or nation at a particular moment.

A word about a possible confusion: The analysis offered here is addressed to differences in the propensity to exert effort due to differences in persons' financial situations and economic opportunities. The analysis is *not* addressed to changes in propensity to exert effort due to previously-exerted effort. For example, the lesser propensity to exert additional effort during the ninth hour of a work day than in the first hour (assuming it to be the case) is not part of this analysis, even though there are obvious links between the two ideas.

Throughout, it is implicitly assumed that all other personal characteristics except wealth are held constant when two wealth states are compared. And specifically, the person is assumed to have the same social class background in both states: comparison of behaviour in different social classes, or of different individuals, is never intended.

Toward A Continuous Consistent Theory

In Becker's analysis of time allocation, the size of the pay-off attached to an opportunity does not affect the work decision as long as the expected pay-off is above the present marginal wage rate. But we know from a variety of evidence that the size of the pay-off *does* matter. Furthermore, a given pay-off will have different effects upon various individuals and nations that work for the same wage. For example, some workers in a given job will accept the offer of overtime work while others will not. Of course we have plenty of *ad hoc* explanations – this one has a date tonight, that one needs extra money because his wife just had another baby. But as Becker (with Michael, 1976) argues particularly strongly, such *ad hoc* explanations leave us unsatisfied because we cannot systematize them with broad general principles, or integrate them with the rest of economic theory.[6] The next chapter aims to make some advance in that direction with regard to the acceptance or rejection of economic opportunities.

This book may be viewed as offering a theory of the formation of the taste for work, where no such theory now exists. Of course this line of analysis does not describe the behaviour of persons for whom the work has evolved into being a pleasure in itself, and where the output of the work is very little used by the worker, such as in science and art.

Notes

1   Hereafter the term 'nation' will be used instead of 'group' unless the subject is a group other than a nation, such as a town or an ethnic or religious community.
2   Throughout the book, the concept of opportunity should be understood as the opportunity *perceived* by the individual or nation, just as for Hicks and Becker wages are assumed to be those known to be available by the individual.
3   There certainly is some relationship among the capacities to exert effort in short contiguous periods, say within a day or even a week or month. And there is common belief in even longer carryover, as expressed in such expressions as 'She is worn out by a hard life'. But I do not know of any scientific evidence on the quantitative nature of such a relationship, or proof that it exists, and therefore a rational person would lack data for

a lifetime allocation. In addition, there are all the uncertainties of life that bedevil a lifetime allocation of wealth with respect to saving and consumption, as well as the issue of discounting. So even if lifetime allocation were an appropriate context for the line of analysis presented here – which it is not – the process would be fraught with grave difficulties.

4 A few notes on the relationship between the Drive–Effort concept as used here, and the common terminology of psychologists: (1) The work activity under discussion here is instrumental rather than consummatory, i.e., persons are assumed to want money for what it will purchase rather than for the sort of gratification misers might get. (2) Historical determinants of behaviour such as habit, learning, and genetic and other structure are assumed the same for the comparisons being made. The only 'internal' condition that varies is wealth, which may be thought of as corresponding to the psychologists' concept of need. (3) The opportunities under discussion are assumed known to the individual or group in question, and have the same probability in all comparisons unless otherwise stated.

A brief outsider's review of the psychological literature on motivation and drive (aside from the physiological level) suggests that there is no consensus on the use of these and related terms, and there is disagreement about whether there might be any meaning in the concepts for which the terms could stand; some theorists suggest that these intervening variables might be done away with completely. But psychologists' disagreements about these concepts in general should not call into question our use of them as intervening variables in this context for two reasons: First, the measures of input (wealth, opportunities) and output (work, innovations, etc.) can be rather well specified in most of the applications we are interested in. Second, it is possible to get independent measures of the intervening drive variable, and this has in fact been done in such studies as Galanter's, when he asked people the effect upon their psyches of various sums of money (described by Stevens, 1959 p. 55). It may be that the relatively clear-cut status of the concept of drive in the context of this paper might offer opportunities for psychologists to exploit in clarifying the theoretical status of the concept.

The reader for whom the relationship between my terminology and that of other scientists is important should take notice of the discussion of 'needs' earlier in this chapter.

5 This model is heavily influenced by Freedman's discussion of values and fertility (1961–2).

6 Becker and Michael put it this way:

For economists to rest a large part of their theory of choice on differences in tastes is disturbing since they admittedly have no useful theory of the formation of tastes, nor can they rely on a well-developed theory of tastes from any other discipline in the social sciences, since none exists. Put differently, the theory which the empirical researcher utilizes is unable to assist him in choosing the appropriate taste proxies on a priori grounds or in formulating predictions about the effects of these variables on behaviour. The weakness in the received theory of choice, then, is the extent to which it relies on differences in tastes to 'explain' behaviour when it can neither explain how tastes are formed nor predict their effects.

To illustrate the reliance on 'changes in tastes' in interpreting observed behaviour, consider the following examples. If a household's utility function has heating fuel as an argument then its tastes must change seasonally to explain why it purchases more fuel in the winter (when the price of fuel is usually higher). Or, couples must experience a shift in preferences toward snow removal services and medical care services and away from sporting goods equipment and high-cholesterol foods as they age since the market prices of these items are not related to age and yet expenditure patterns appear to change with the couple's age. Of course, by incorporating an intuitively appealing explanation in each case, economists usually interpret these observations in reasonable ways. The important point, however, is that the received theory of choice itself is of modest use in that undertaking. (In Becker, 1976, p. 133)

4

The Drive–Effort Hypothesis

It is time to state the Drive–Effort hypothesis more precisely. The pay-off to an alternative may be defined as

$$(W_{n+1}^{\text{yes}} - W_n) - (W_{n+1}^{\text{no}} - W_n)$$

where 'yes' and 'no' mean respectively that the opportunity will or will not be undertaken, $n+1$ and n indicate the states before and after the alternative would be carried out, and W stands for wealth (including otherwise-expected lifetime income) divided by expected years of life. This pay-off definition may be shortened to $(W_{n+1} - W_n)$ for convenience, on the assumption of no change otherwise.

It is reasonable that Drive–Effort – or the expected strength of response to an opportunity, if one prefers to view the matter that way – depends upon (a) the pay-off per unit of work time, and (b) the individual's or nation's wealth. The effect of the expected pay-off is obvious without examples. The effect of wealth becomes equally obvious with a few simple examples such as: (a) In a subsistence-agriculture economy, one does not build a house for oneself if one already has a house. (b) You do not prepare a meal if you have one already prepared. (c) Campers only work at setting up camp until it is set up. In these primitive examples, wealth in the widest sense obviously affects the supply of work. Hopefully, this observation is enough to establish the point, though the desire for money to buy goods seems less specific than the desire for specific goods, and the marginal utility of money does not so obviously decrease as does the marginal utility of additional goods.

It does not seem reasonable, however, that the simple difference between W_{n+1} and W_n, written $(W_{n+1} - W_n)$, indicates the strength of the desire for money, or of Drive–Effort; a millionaire will not perform the same acts to get an additional dollar as will a pauper, on average; rather, it is reasonable to think that the difference is seen relative to the individual's wealth, assuming that the net money flow is positive and that the opportunity offers a pay-off higher than the value of time in Becker's reckoning. Therefore, I propose the formulation

Drive–Effort Measure = expected likelihood of positive
response to a given opportunity
by individual or nation

$$= a \left(\frac{W_{n+1} - W_n}{W_n} \right)$$

which takes the exponential form shown in figure 4.1. The function has the property that a doubling of wealth leads to a halving of Drive–Effort, where wealth refers to the person's situation with and without the opportunity in question, and therefore the function's value changes as a person does more and more work. That is, Drive–Effort is proportional to $(W_{n+1} - W_n)$ at any given level of initial wealth, and it is inversely proportional to W_n, as may be seen in figure 4.1, and at subsequent wealth positions; this will be made clearer in the monopoly–duopoly analysis in chapter 6. But the theory does not require any particular relationship (other than monotonicity) between opportunity and Effort.

The effort that one *would* expend must be distinguished from the effort that one *must* expend in order actually to undertake a given opportunity. The DrEf Measure defined above refers to the amount of effort a person *would* expend for a given pay-off. If the effort actually *required* for a given alternative is below the Drive–Effort Measure for that alternative at a given level of wealth, the opportunity will be accepted; if not, not. For example, assume that the level of effort *required* for a particular opportunity Z is shown by the horizontal line Z in figure 4.1. At all wealth positions producing at least the effort required for Z or more, the alternative Z will be undertaken.

This formulation has attractions in addition to its plausibility and

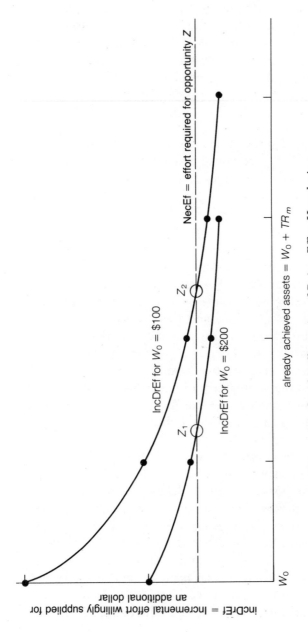

Figure 4.1 Graphic illustration of Drive–Effort Hypothesis

Principle of construction: $IncDrEf = \dfrac{(TR_{m+1} + W_0) - (TR_m + W_0)}{(TR_m + W_0)}$

where TR_m = total revenue obtained from efforts until now
TR_{m+1} = total revenue from efforts until now plus another unit of effort
W_0 = initial endowment
IncDrEf = effort willingly supplied for another dollar

simplicity. First, it corresponds to the classic Weber–Fechner Law in psychophysics, according to which the likelihood of response to a given difference in stimuli is proportional to the lower level of the stimuli. Second, the function may be seen as an operationalization of the standard logarithmic conception (when viewed cumulatively) of (Benthamite) diminishing marginal utility of money.[1] (The two functions are in fact one and the same, but viewed in different ways.) And of course this shape of function is consistent with the conventional assumption of concave indifference curves between pairs of goods. It should also be noted that there is some empirical support for a semi-logarithmic utility function, for example, in Galanter's study that asked questions about the respondent's speculations about his or her own happiness in connection with various levels of wealth.[2]

The Drive–Effort Measure might be better represented with some other concave-downwards function. The power function is one such candidate (as has been suggested in some psychophysical experiments), and there may be others. But the particular function is not of crucial importance; only its downward-concavity matters, or even just its downward slope.

The relationship of the Drive–Effort concept to the concept of diminishing marginal utility of money suggests that we look into the meaning of the latter for our purposes here. That concept suggests that a given increment of money is 'worth' less when one is richer. But how does one measure an increment's 'worth' except by evaluating what a person will trade for it? And the only exchange that might provide grounds for analysis would be a non-market good, because money has no economic meaning except as power to purchase goods. (Conceivably, one might measure the amounts that rich and poor persons would pay for food or water on a lifeboat, but this would be neither an easy test nor a very meaningful one, for a variety of reasons.) It seems reasonable, however, to measure the utility of money according to the time and effort that people will give up to get it, and the goods that it will purchase.[3] If so, the utility and the effort become operationally indistinguishable, though some persons may wish to continue thinking of them as separate concepts.

One may also measure the utility of money (really, the utility of goods) with such questions as how happy an additional sum would make one, or with the probability of suicide connected with various wealth (income) levels.[4] But such measurements seem more relevant for making income redistributions than for predicting how various persons will behave in the face of various opportunities, which is our subject here (Simon, 1974).

The relationship between wealth and effort implies a cyclical effect: lack of wealth leads to effort, effort leads to wealth, wealth leads to lack of effort, lack of effort leads to lack of wealth. This is similar to the cycle described by 'shirtsleeves to shirtsleeves in three generations'. But this cycle need not suggest a trap of economic stagnation, for at least three reasons. First, the advance of technology (itself a result of effort) enables successive generations to live better at a given level of effort. Second, it may be that there is a *relative* wealth effect (see Brenner, 1983) which causes people at a given level of absolute wealth to exert more effort if the wealth of others is higher, *ceteris paribus*, and makes one feel poorer; this also could be explained in absolute wealth terms, however, if higher observed wealth of others increases perceived opportunities, and hence induces more effort. Third, as a society becomes more wealthy, new profitable opportunities arise, the promise of which may induce effort in individuals whose personal wealth would keep them from exerting effort to exploit the less attractive opportunities available in a poorer society.

The types of decisions discussed here could conceivably be crammed within the framework of the pure logic of choice. But if that were to be done, there would be no gain in understanding the particular forces that affect the choices, an understanding of which is vital for many economic analyses.

Specification and Measurement of Key Concepts

If this theory is to be useful, one must be able to measure its key variables. Despite the earlier discussion of the possible direct measurement of utility, the Drive–Effort concept never needs to be measured in practice; the discussion of utility measurement was for expository purposes only.

The measurement of wealth is straightforward though it may not be easy. The individual's (or family's or group's) assets, as valued in market prices, constitute an appropriate measure in most cases. In some other cases, the person's expected stream of earnings may be the appropriate concept, and the stream may often be estimated with characteristics such as education that are related to income, as human capital theory teaches. In some cases an appropriate measure of wealth may not be obvious, and will require hard thought and serious justification. But in principle, the measurement of wealth presents no problem. (The measurement of *relative* wealth and the role of that factor are discussed further in the section on income distribution in chapter 8.)

The reasons *why* people want money – for its purchasing power, its status effect, its sense of security, or others – do not matter for the analysis presented here. All that matters is that a person's wealth in money can be measured, and that the added wealth offered by an opportunity can also be measured.

The measurement of opportunity may often be difficult. Some cases are straightforward, though, such as (a) increasing the payment offered for an evening's overtime work; (b) increasing the reward offered to a commercial diver who hesitates to descend to a dangerous depth; (c) offering a reward to a Delhi pedicab driver for getting the rider to the destination before a specified hour.

The income effect causes difficulty in measuring a change in opportunity and its effects. A physician's move from the Philippines to the United States assuredly increases the physician's opportunity, but the income effect may reduce the amount and intensity of work exerted by the physician.

A price reduction, or the equivalent of a price reduction in the guise of the onset of availability of a product to a group or individual, raises perhaps the most complex issues of specification and measurement. Such a phenomenon has offsetting impacts through the channels of changes in both wealth and opportunity, analogous to the income and substitution effects in demand analysis. For example, if the tax on automobiles in the Soviet Union were to be removed and the price lowered, people would suddenly be more wealthy because their financial assets would enable them to own a good that was previously unobtainable by them, thereby leading to a reduction in Drive–Effort. On the other hand, the lower price would represent an increase in opportunity, because any given amount of additional earnings would institute an increased opportunity to own an auto, thereby inducing an increase in DrEf. Another example is the increased availability of consumer goods in the early stage of economic development. The net effect, and hence the outcome of the two impacts, would seem to be indeterminate in these cases, though perhaps further analysis of lifetime income (including present wealth) would produce an unambiguous predicted effect.

The form in which the Drive–Effort hypothesis is currently stated will lack aesthetic appeal for economists, because it is not now framed in terms of utility maximization. But there is no reason to doubt that further work can forge that connection with microeconomic theory, just as has occurred with such ideas as mean-variance analysis that were originally stated in a form disconnected from other theory.

Notes

1 The concept of utility referred to in this essay harks back to the original Benthamite concept. In the writing of Bentham and his followers, 'utility' referred to ex post happiness and pleasure, and was frankly psychological. Economists gradually purged the term of its pleasure-pain psychological content, culminating in the work of Slutsky (1951) and von Neumann-Morgenstern (1947) in which utility became an unobservable ex ante magnitude that was theoretically useful to postulate as a foundation for a consistent, positive choice theory. This book returns to the original Benthamic meaning of the term.

Much confusion also has arisen because of the shift over the years in the use of the concept of utility, from the theory of public policy to the theory of choice. When the utility concept was introduced by Bentham, the subject of discussion was legislation and governance. The 'moral arithmetic' of utility was intended to promote wise laws and human social structure. But economists have come to use 'utility theory to *explain* economic behaviour (particularly demand theory) and only secondarily (when at all) to amend or justify economic policy' (Stigler, 1965, p. 67). The distinction between the two uses has frequently been blurred or overlooked, which has led to great confusion. This footnote is drawn from my 1974 article.

Nothing said here implies that I advocate a utilitarian framework for evaluating social policies.

2 Described by Stevens (1959, pp. 54–5).

3 As Marshall put it:

If the desires to secure either of two pleasures will induce people in similar circumstances each to do just an hour's extra work, or will induce men in the same rank of life and with the same means each

to pay a shilling for it; we then may say that those pleasures are
equal for our purposes, because the desires for them are equally
strong incentives to action for persons under similar conditions.
(1920, p. 16)

This suggests that whatever two persons in *different* circumstances will
each sacrifice a *given* amount of time to attain has the same value for the
two of them.

4   For a review of such material, see Simon (1974).

5

Relevant Data and Suggested Tests

This chapter presents data showing that the Drive–Effort Measure influences economic behaviour. The data make especially clear that poorer people will expend more time and effort to increase their economic position than will richer people. The chapter also discusses types of data which could falsify the hypothesis if collected in future research.

The data that are presented do not 'prove' the Drive–Effect hypothesis. But taken together, they would seem to accord the hypothesis sufficient credibility so that it should be considered seriously.

Many of the citations in this chapter are derived from my earlier work on quite different topics. This suggests that there is likely to be a large volume of other relevant studies and data which I have not fallen upon in the course of other sorts of excursions, and which the research for this volume has not yet turned up. I will be grateful for suggestions about other relevant materials.

Industrial Payment Systems

Schemes of payments to industrial workers vary in the extent to which they are directly tied to the individual's output. Therefore, the systems differ in the opportunities available for the individual to increase his or her purchasing power. Economic theory seems to be silent about the relationship between the effort exerted and the scheme by which a person is paid – flat wage, individual piecework, group piecework, etc. (For the recent state of thought and some evidence, see Hamermesh and Rees, 1984, pp. 51 and 52.) The Drive–Effort hypothesis, however, implies that because the relationship between effort exerted and pay received is closer in a piecework scheme than in a flat wage scheme, the former should elicit more effort than the latter – a proposition which seems quite commonsensical but has not hitherto been proven rigorously, to my knowledge.

Pencavel (1977) focuses upon a different mechanism than property-rights incentive in his analysis of the modes of payment and their results. He sensibly suggests that employers are willing to pay workers more with a piece-rate system than with a time-rate system because less supervision is needed with a piece-rate system, with a consequent saving to the employer; he calls the latter an 'on-the-job screening system'. One might add that the greater consistency from week to week of worker output under a piece-rate system (as documented in studies referred to below) also could be a benefit to employers. Seiler (1984, table 2) found a bit more supervision for time workers than for incentive workers in the footwear industry (0.7 versus 0.6), but *much less* supervision for time workers in the men's and boys' suits-and-coats industry (0.02 versus 0.07); which runs against Pencavel's hypothesis. The much larger standard deviation for time workers suggests that this latter comparison may be erroneous, however.

If Pencavel is correct, one would expect the payments to workers to be proportionally greater under a piece-rate system than the proportional increase in productivity; this would be consistent with lower costs of supervision under a piece-rate system. I do not know of any data testing this, however, so Pencavel's hypothesis must be considered as consistent with the data, but no more consistent with it than other explanations.

It should be noted that even if Pencavel's explanation is fully supported, it would not be inconsistent with a property-rights incentive explanation of worker behaviour. Rather, it simply suggests that a piece-rate system motivates with money whereas a time-rate system motivates with fear of supervisory action.

Hamermesh and Rees suggest another mechanism which is consistent with a property-rights incentive explanation, that workers are self-selected to work in a piece-rate system. If so, there is no difference in effort by the same sort of person to be explained by the mode of payment. By the same token, the self-selection explanation is not inconsistent with Pencavel's on-the-job screening system.

Before beginning on the systematic evidence, here are a few anecdotal accounts:

> (1) Southern Utah Fuel Company's workforce is largely Mormon, as is its management.

> Partly because Sufco's workers are so devoted to the company, they dig an astounding 2½ times more coal per man per day than is dug in the average underground coal mine in the US. That is good for the mine, of course, and the workers enlarge their salaries by cashing in on production incentives.[1]

> (2)

> Lots of companies these days are huffing and puffing to find some good way to motivate workers. Lincoln Electric Co. found the way it wanted in 1907 and says it has liked the results ever since.

> The company relies on incentives. It pays most of its 2,500 employees on a piecework basis. In 1933, it added an annual bonus system. Based on performance, bonuses may exceed regular pay, and they apply far more extensively than in most companies. A secretary's mistakes, for example, can cut her bonus.

> Some employees complain of pressure. But they stay around. Turnover is only 0.3% a month. The Cleveland company has no unions, and it avoids strikes. It says employees have *averaged* as much as $45,000 a year in good times. Sales and earnings have risen at a respectable pace.[2]

> (3)

> [W]here pay-for-performance has been universally and rigorously applied, it has often had dramatic results. Frank Schultz, a BankAmerica senior vice-president, runs the company's credit card division. He has put all of his 3,500 employees under a pay-for-performance system, which ranks them against their peers, using 200 specific criteria. 'I measure everything that moves', Mr. Schultz says.[3]

The following types of systematic studies show that the expected effect of incentive plans is indeed observed:

(1) In eight auto-repair occupations

Workers in auto dealer repair shops who were paid under incentive plans nearly always averaged more per hour than those paid time rates, according to a Bureau of Labor Statistics survey of 36 metropolitan areas in June 1973. Typically, the incentive-paid workers earned 20 to 50 percent more per hour than their time-rated counterparts.

With only one exception (lubrication workers in San Francisco), incentive-paid workers averaged more than time-rated workers in the same occupation wherever both systems were used. [See table 5.1] The earnings differentials varied widely, however, among occupations within an area and for an occupation compared across areas.

(King, 1975, pp. 45–6)

(2) Rothe (1951, p. 96, and earlier publications cited there) suggested that consistency of performance is a sensible measure of the 'effectiveness of incentives'. It seems reasonable that great fluctuation in a worker's performance from period to period indicates a relatively low level of effort, given the concept of effort that is under discussion here. Rothe (p. 94) compared 16 weeks of output rates for (a) chocolate dippers in a candy factory who were 'paid a one-to-one ratio for performance over standard', against (b) the output records of butter wrappers and machine operators, neither of whom were paid on the basis of performance. The correlation from week to week for the chocolate dippers ($r = 0.85$) was much higher than for the other two types of workers – an 'enormous range' for butter wrappers, and $r = 0.57$ and 0.68 from fortnight to fortnight for the machine operators. Rothe also cited a study by Tiffin (1942) which showed a very high week-to-week correlation coefficient ($r = 0.96$) for hosiery loopers, who were paid on an 'incentive system'.

(3) Kilbridge (1960) went beyond Rothe's idea to suggest that effective incentives not only reduce variation from period to period for the individual worker, but also tend to reduce variation *among* workers. And he displayed the distributions of

Table 5.1 Average hourly earnings in dollars of incentive workers compared with averages for time-rated workers in auto dealer repair shops, selected areas, June 1973

Area	Body repairers		Lubrication employees		Journeymen automotive mechanics		Automotive service mechanics		New-car get-ready employees		Painters		Parts employees		Service salesworkers	
	Earn-ings	Rela-tive	Earn-ings	Rela-tive	Earn-ings	Rela-tive	Earn-ings	Rela-tive	Earn-ings	Rela-tive	Earn-ings	Rela-tive	Earn-ings	Rela-tive	Earn-ings	Rela-tive
North East																
Boston	6.78	151	4.79	162	6.66	144	4.90	129	5.15	129	6.09	148	4.60	125	5.14	117
Bridgeport	6.64	141	–	–	5.84	130	4.68	130	–	–	–	–	4.92	129	5.63	132
Buffalo	5.47	111	4.20	139	5.25	–	4.02	135	5.06	145	6.16	–	4.65	136	4.74	135
Nassau-Suffolk	6.44	133	3.83	103	6.68	117	4.86	121	5.31	148	5.33	125	5.02	143	5.59	116
Newark	6.12	126	5.73	193	6.38	140	3.88	115	4.34	133	–	–	4.69	129	5.13	122
New York	6.91	142	4.60	124	6.59	126	4.77	111	5.07	125	6.46	151	5.10	129	5.79	135
Philadelphia	5.55	134	–	–	6.16	153	4.81	142	4.86	161	6.25	155	4.95	150	5.08	122
Pittsburgh	5.98	164	–	–	5.55	143	4.55	129	4.92	153	–	–	4.42	151	5.25	133
Providence-Pawtucket-Warwick	5.49	128	3.79	150	5.08	125	4.15	133	5.84	175	–	–	3.55	118	4.02	112
South																
Atlanta	6.99	–	5.71	208	6.50	–	5.44	–	4.99	152	7.75	–	4.74	122	6.96	–
Baltimore	6.61	–	–	–	6.02	–	4.71	139	4.71	155	6.38	151	3.63	120	4.69	117
Birmingham	5.75	–	4.52	–	5.71	–	5.22	–	–	–	5.67	–	4.24	124	4.82	–
Dallas	6.82	–	4.42	198	5.68	123	5.51	164	6.35	205	6.43	166	4.95	154	5.58	116
Houston	6.74	–	6.15	257	6.46	153	4.46	138	6.14	185	6.86	–	5.35	172	5.89	158
Jacksonville	5.97	–	4.14	–	5.69	–	5.46	–	4.87	181	5.78	–	4.92	142	6.08	160
Louisville	5.63	–	5.27	–	5.39	–	3.66	–	5.22	198	6.38	–	4.01	126	5.59	140
Memphis	6.31	–	4.15	222	5.23	–	3.81	–	–	–	6.03	138	4.97	171	4.88	–
Miami	7.43	–	5.30	196	6.97	–	6.12	–	5.57	176	7.55	–	4.61	132	5.95	–
New Orleans	5.64	–	3.76	–	5.28	–	4.57	–	4.51	179	6.71	–	4.15	141	5.11	164
Richmond	5.80	–	–	–	5.35	–	–	–	3.77	131	7.75	–	4.01	136	4.43	126

Table 5.1 Continued

Area	Body repairers Earnings	Body repairers Relative	Lubrication employees Earnings	Lubrication employees Relative	Journeymen automotive mechanics Earnings	Journeymen automotive mechanics Relative	Automotive service mechanics Earnings	Automotive service mechanics Relative	New-car get-ready employees Earnings	New-car get-ready employees Relative	Painters Earnings	Painters Relative	Parts employees Earnings	Parts employees Relative	Service salesworkers Earnings	Service salesworkers Relative
Tampa-St Petersburg	5.88	–	5.34	208	6.33	–	4.55	137	4.52	152	5.39	177	3.91	140	4.88	135
Washington	8.08	–	–	–	6.67	136	4.52	117	–	–	8.17	194	4.42	127	5.79	127
North Central																
Chicago	8.54	144	5.27	150	7.87	130	–	–	8.34	200	8.49	116	5.22	122	5.67	107
Cincinnati	6.42	–	3.21	123	5.75	–	–	–	4.79	159	6.73	–	4.04	128	4.97	162
Cleveland	7.26	–	4.70	137	7.16	–	4.75	114	7.90	191	7.90	–	4.74	140	5.33	120
Detroit	8.35	–	5.58	193	7.51	–	6.01	162	6.77	161	9.24	–	4.92	136	5.12	121
Indianapolis	6.41	–	5.04	160	5.77	178	5.58	173	6.41	191	6.68	–	3.33	105	4.81	127
Kansas City	6.53	–	5.62	205	6.37	–	5.86	–	6.18	150	7.50	–	4.92	115	5.62	137
Milwaukee	6.61	–	5.39	184	6.28	–	4.79	133	4.85	157	6.81	–	4.72	174	4.75	129
Minneapolis-St Paul	6.73	141	5.77	169	6.66	135	7.03	167	5.36	131	8.50	–	4.44	113	5.39	135
St Louis	7.68	138	7.41	150	6.91	125	–	–	5.80	107	8.72	–	5.84	111	6.85	121
West																
Denver	6.56	–	5.74	–	6.70	–	4.80	124	4.79	144	7.90	–	4.89	159	5.16	152
Los Angeles-Long Beach	6.75	–	6.45	–	6.86	145	5.27	137	5.45	149	7.80	–	4.74	126	6.48	120
Portland	6.16	120	–	–	6.32	135	4.28	–	4.35	122	5.35	–	4.25	113	4.85	137
San Francisco-Oakland	–	–	4.09	85	7.00	107	–	–	–	–	–	–	6.56	122	6.38	103
Seattle-Everett	–	–	–	–	–	–	–	–	–	–	–	–	–	–	–	–

Average hourly earnings for time-rated workers = 100

Dashes indicate no data reported, data that do not meet publication criteria, or insufficient data to compare time and incentive earnings output relative to the mean output for two incentive schemes, of which he considered one to be effective and one ineffective, data which he takes as confirming his hypothesis (his tables 1 and 2). The 'ineffective' plan was used in machining departments, whereas the 'effective' plan was used in a clerical department; in principle, this difference in locus could be responsible for some or all of the difference in distributions, but Kilbridge apparently did not think it was so.

On the other hand, Hamermesh and Rees (1984, p. 52) expect that 'the distribution of total earnings is much wider within a narrow industry among workers who receive incentive pay than among those paid by the hour'. Seiler (1984) analysed data on over 100,000 workers in 500 firms making 'footwear' and 'men's and boys' suits and coats', and found more dispersion among earning of piece-rate workers than among time workers. This seems to be a very careful piece of work using a large sample and effective statistical controls, and therefore probably deserves more confidence than does Kilbridge's earlier study.

(4) Seiler (1984) offers solid evidence that incentive workers earn more – 14 per cent more – than do time workers. And after allowing for 'risk' (in the form of dispersion of earnings) he finds that the 'effort earnings hypothesis' explains most of the difference in earning under the two systems (p. 375).

Perhaps the most careful study of time-rate versus piece-rate systems is Pencavel's analysis (1977) of the data collected by Rees and Schultz (1970) in Chicago. He held constant such human-capital factors as schooling, and found that workers paid by the piece earned 7 per cent more per hour. He did not, however, show that piece-rated workers *produced more* per hour, and if his analysis of the economics of payment modes is correct, productivity could be less different (or no different) than earnings. But taken together with other studies, it seems reasonable to conclude that productivity as well as pay is higher in a piece-rate system.

(5) Weinstein and Holzbach (1973) compared, in a laboratory setting using college students as subjects, the effects of two payment plans: (a) an 'individual' incentive plan – actually, different proportions of their three-person group's total payments, depending on their relative performance within the

group, the group's earnings being a direct function of output; and (b) a group incentive plan – all three members of the group receiving equal shares of the group's earnings. Production was higher with individual incentives. Weinstein and Holzbach also split the groups into what they call high and low 'task-flow interdependence', a measure of how an individual work rate depends upon how fast the other persons are processing their work. (This is actually the case only for the second and third workers in the group, though the first worker in the flow sees his or her effect upon the others, presumably.) Low interdependence yields higher productivity than does high interdependence. The order of the groups from best to worst performance (aside from a possible reversal with respect to the most highly qualified workers, in the individual reward condition) is: individual incentive–low interdependence; group–low, individual–high; and group–high. These results are consistent with expectations concerning the effect of payment system upon effort.

(6) Farr (1976) added two conditions to the Weinstein–Holzbach design: no incentive at all, and pure individual incentive. The main result is that all incentive plans do better than plans with no incentive. The group incentive does slightly better than the combined incentive, which in turn does slightly better than the individual incentive.

Terborg and Miller (1978) compared piece-rate versus hourly pay in a laboratory experiment with students. The quantity produced was higher with piece rates. Quality may have been lower, but the result was not statistically significant. If quality was indeed lower, overall value of production may not have been greater with piece rates.

It is interesting that psychologists have found it necessary to conduct laboratory experiments (and on-the-job studies, as reviewed above) to establish the existence of what would seem to be a commonsensical idea. This is in part because various theories concerning 'equity' and job satisfaction have suggested that the commonsensical view is inadequate. And, according to Farr (p. 159), 'The theoretical base for much of this research has been operant conditioning'. Whatever the merit of these contrary speculations, the pure incentive effect seems to dominate empirically.

In the Weinstein–Holzbach and Farr experiments, in the

group-incentive treatments the rest of the group presumably knows the performance of each individual. This knowledge could affect performance, and indeed, could account for the group incentive plan doing as well as the individual incentive plan. It is a fact of life that the regard of one's fellows is an important reward, and the desire for it is an important incentive. Therefore, we must consider those experiments as having two jointly-working incentive systems. Examining the two systems together may yield appropriate information for decision-makers studying which alternative plan to adopt. But that jointness muddies the waters as we seek to learn about the effects of opportunity upon effort.

(7) Another group of experiments compares (implicitly) the effect of incentives that are more dependent versus those that are less dependent upon one's own productivity when the rest of the group presumably has little or no knowledge of each individual's output. In group rope-pulling, and in group shouting and clapping, the size of the co-operating group has an inverse relationship upon the per-person effort expended (Maital, 1982, pp. 126, 127). One may wonder why a person will exert *any* effort if one's output is unknown. Game-theoretic notions come into play here. But it may also be that in these experiments, individuals did not believe that their output would be completely unknown to others, and therefore they did not try to be completely-free riders. It would be interesting to push this line of research even further by designing experiments wherein the individual's output is known to a varying degree by others, ranging from full knowledge down to no knowledge at all.

(8) More generally, a wide-ranging review by Locke et al. (1980) of a large number of studies found money payment schemes to be 'the most successful techniques for motivating employees', compared to 'job enrichment', 'goal setting', 'participation', and the like. These results must be seen as something of a blow to social theorists who have hoped that restructuring society could induce high productivity without the 'capitalist' methods that depend upon what is often called 'greed'.

This section should not be taken as an endorsement of particular piecework incentive schemes in industry, because group pressures can operate to subvert the scheme. As noted by Lupton and Cunnison after a study of three piecework plans in the United Kingdom:

> If an operative, or a group of operatives, observes that the relationship between the effort they exert, and the cash reward they receive, is affected by factors which are beyond their control, it seems natural that they will attempt to redress the balance by operating such controls as are open to them. Depending on circumstances one may find attempts to 'fiddle' on booking, on quality, or on work allocation. The extent to which these efforts are successful will depend upon factors peculiar to each workshop; such as the strength of Trade Union organisation, the degree of machine pacing of the process, and the like. (1957, p. 269)

One should notice, however, the underlying assumption made by those authors that effort can be influenced by the payment scheme.

Hours Worked

Wealth and Hours Worked

Though the amount of data pertaining to work *time* that are reviewed here is relatively large compared to the amount of data on work *intensity*, one should not be misled into thinking that the DrEf hypothesis refers mostly to the time aspect of effort.[4] Rather, *intensity* of work effort is probably the more important and certainly the more interesting aspect of the phenomenon, both with respect to the magnitude of effort as a variable and also in the power of the DrEf hypothesis to explain and predict economic behaviour.

The data connecting wealth and hours worked may be explained by Becker's time theory. But they also are consistent with the Drive–Effort hypothesis, which is why they are presented here. (The data presented on hours worked with respect to variables *other* than wealth pertain *only* to the Drive–Effort hypothesis, and not to Becker's theory, as is the case with the data on work intensity.)

(1) Kindleberger (1965) plotted the logarithm of hours of

work in manufacturing in 1961 against wealth (actually income)[5] and found a very clear-cut relationship, as seen in figure 5.1. And from similar data Winston (1966) estimated an elasticity of −0.1.

(2) Data for non-agricultural weekly work hours in the United States starting in 1870 show a strong inverse wealth-hours relationship until well after the Second World War (figure 5.2), though work-week hours apparently stabilize sometime after that. Becker suggests that the apparent stabilization is due to changes in the time-intensity of the baskets of goods that consumers have purchased over the years, and if this is true, the absence of relationship in the recent period does not falsify the hypothesized wealth-work relationship. However, Rees (1979) suggests that the apparent stabilization of 'average' work-week hours may be an artefact, because people may be reducing the number of weeks worked per year, and thereby reducing total

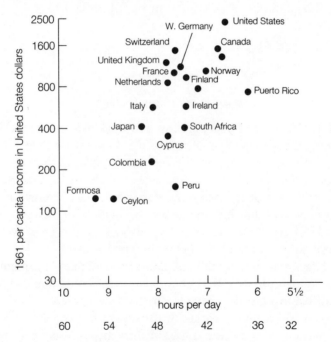

Figure 5.1 Hours of work in manufacturing per week in a cross-section of countries,
1961
Source: Kindleberger, 1965, p.6

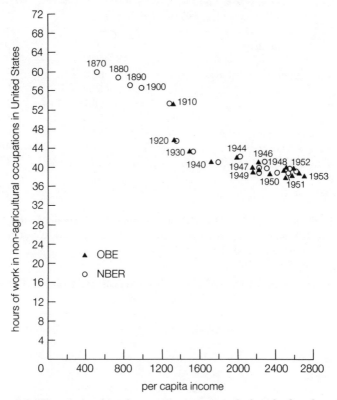

Figure 5.2 The relationship of per-capita income to the length of work week in non-agricultural occupations in the United States, 1870–1960
Sources: Work week, De Grazia, 1962, table 1; per capita income, Historical Statistics of the U.S. *Reproduced from Simon, 1977, p. 60*

hours worked over the year, even though reported 'representative' work-week hours remain unchanged.

The data in table 5.2 showing the increasing trend in the United States in lost workdays due to ailments from 1973 to 1980 support that supposition (especially since fatalities do *not* rise, as Hamermesh has mentioned). And the data in table 5.3 show that during the period 1957 to 1971 for which data are available, effective working time in West Germany declined much more than did paid working time.

Table 5.4 shows the effective working time in various

Table 5.2   Lost workdays from occupational illness or injury, incidence per 100 full-time workers, by industry, 1973 and 1980

Industry	1973	1980
Agriculture, forestry, and fishing	68.0	82.7
Mining	119.6	163.6
Construction	98.1	117.0
Manufacturing	68.2	86.7
Transportation and public utilities	82.5	104.5
Wholesale and retail trade	37.6	48.7
Finance, insurance, and real estate	10.2	12.2
Services	27.5	35.8
Total private sector	53.3	65.2

Source: Hamermesh and Rees (1984), p. 285. Originally, *Handbook of Labor Statistics, 1980*, table 175, and *Occupational Injuries and Illnesses in the United States by Industry, 1980*, Bulletin no. 2130, table 1

Table 5.3   Average working time of industrial workers (male and female) in West Germany in hours per week

Year	Paid working time[a]	Effective working time
1947	39.1	–
1948	42.4	–
1949	46.5	–
1950	48.2	–
1951	47.5	–
1952	47.6	–
1953	47.9	–
1954	48.6	–
1955	48.8	–
1956	48.0	–
1957	46.5	43.0
1958	45.7	41.5
1959	45.6	41.3
1960	45.6	42.0
1961	45.5	40.8
1962	44.9	40.8
1963	44.7	40.2
1964	44.1	41.1

Table 5.3 Continued

Year	Paid working time[a]	Effective working time
1965	44.3	40.2
1966	43.9	40.1
1967	42.3	39.6
1968	43.3	39.2
1969	44.0	39.7
1970	44.0	37.4
1971	43.2	37.4
1972	42.8	–
1973	42.8	–
1974	41.9	–
1975	40.5	–
1976	41.6	–
1977	41.7	–
1978	41.6	–
1979	41.9	–
1980	41.6	–
1981	41.2	–
1982	40.7	–
1983	40.5	–

Source: Statistisches Jahrbuch der Bundesrepublik Deutschland, Statistisches Bundesamt, ed., different years, compiled by Andreas Blomenkamp
[a]Working time and time which accounts towards working time (vacation, illness, etc.)

European countries for 1970 to 1981, for completeness of presentation as well as for general interest.

It has not been easy to establish the relationship of wealth to work hours net of the effects of wages and standardized by income, age, and other relevant variables in micro-level data. Smith (1977) argues, for example, that studies relating hours of work to assets in a one-period framework will produce misleading results (he refers to several such studies which he says are flawed in this respect), and he suggests that the subject needs to be studied in a life-cycle framework; Smith also shows that, contrary to expectations, the coefficient for net worth's effect on hours of work is *positive* for both men and women in

Table 5.4 Effective working time in industry per worker (hours per year)

Country	1970	1972	1973	1974	1975	1976	1977	1978	1979	1980	1981
W. Germany	1885	1827	1814	1775	1731	1781	1755	1731	1721	17 6	1685
France	2044	2010	1989	1959	1913	1911	1894	1881	1874	1860	1847
Great Britain	2018	1969	2008	1952	1930	1936	1955	1952	1948	1895	1865
Netherlands	2041	1859	1827	1769	1736	1731	1726	1715	1698	1655	–
Belgium	2075	2012	1955	1903	1810	1862	1825	1830	1841	1835	–
United States	1903	1937	1940	1903	1884	1900	1904	1907	1902	1888	1888
Japan	2252	2200	2184	2080	2018	2090	2096	2106	2128	2132	2123
Austria	1945	1893	1872	1872	1763	1789	1768	1736	1744	1751	1710
Switzerland	1918	1905	1901	1892	1841	1905	1915	1905	1896	1890	1878
Sweden	1744	1694	1662	1644	1610	1590	1578	1558	1533	1506	1500

Source: Hof, B. and Vajna, Th. 'Arbeitszeitpolitik in der Bundesrepublik Deutschland' in Wirtschafts- und Gesellschafts politische Grundinformationen, no. 55, 5/1983

the 1967 Survey of Economic Opportunity (SEO) data. But this finding does not vitiate the findings of an inverse relationship in national time series or cross-sections, because most of the bias to which Smith alerts us should wash out in aggregate analysis. And such difficulties have not made it impossible to draw some persuasive conclusions from the many other studies that have been made. Killingsworth (1983) has, with seeming care, reviewed and summarized the large body of micro-level studies (as well as many aggregate time-series studies) of the relationship of wealth to quantity of work, both static and dynamic labor-supply models. He confidently concluded as follows: "There is now a great deal of empirical evidence about labor supply behavior. First, and of crucial importance, pecuniary variables – wage rates and property income [the latter being the wealth variable of interest here] – do generally seem to have something to do with labor supply." (p. 432) That is, greater wealth leads to less work being supplied.

(3) Men with working wives moonlight less than men whose wives do not work (Guthrie, 1966). A working wife is an important economic asset; the man whose wife works is effectively richer than the man whose wife does not, and hence it is consistent with the hypothesis that the former works less than the latter.

(4) Men with 'disorderly work histories' moonlight more than do other men (Guthrie, 1966). A man with little job security has poorer prospects in present-value terms than does the man whose job is secure, and hence it makes sense in terms of the Drive–Effort hypothesis that he works more.

(5) Even *subjective* poverty leads a person to work more. Wilensky (1963) found that men who feel less well off than their parents are more likely to moonlight.

(6) Shisko and Rostker (1976) explored the effects of moonlighting in a thorough multivariate fashion. Though moonlighters have less income from assets than do non-moonlighters, on average, and though the wealth term is negative in their multivariate analysis, it is not statistically significant. This study, however, may also fall victim to the statistical difficulty pointed out by Smith, mentioned just above.

(7) Using a national probability sample of working males

drawn by the Survey Research Center of the Institute for Social Research at the University of Michigan in 1975, Filer investigated the relationship between non-wage income and the extent which people responded positively to this question:

> Now I'd like you to think of a 10-point scale for the amount of *energy* and *effort* you put into an activity, with 10 representing *all* your energy and effort, and 0 representing hardly any at all. Five would be about half-way in between. I'm going to read you a list of activities and you tell me what number you would give it.   (Filer, 1986)

The correlation was not statistically significant when a variety of other background variables were held constant. But the absence of relationship could be caused by at least two factors: (1) Relative unimportance of the variable 'non-wage income', which does not include the effects of the wealth of home ownership, probably the most important wealth for most wage workers; (2) Inappropriateness of the question for our purposes here. To expect a relationship presumes that workers would believe more effort would lead to a higher pay-off by way of higher wages. This qualification is supported by the fact that a regression of wages on reported effort did not show a significant relationship. Also, the question gets at effort *actually exerted*, which can be increased by age or disability or lack of skill, rather than being the effort the person *would be willing* to exert for increased income.

Filer's inquiry is mentioned here less because of the data than because it points toward how valuable work might be done on this topic with better data.

Filer also investigated a similar relationship with hours of work as the dependent variable. Here he found a significant negative relationship between non-wage income and hours, as well as a positive relationship between the number of children and the number of hours, as one would expect.

Transfer Payments and Hours Worked

One of the great perennial social questions is the effect of various sorts of welfare and transfer payments upon the recipient's propensity to work; the underlying idea, of course, is that the wealth bestowed by the payments decreases Drive–Effort. The negative income tax experiments in the United States were intended to answer this question better than other sorts of evidence that had been adduced in the past.

The results of those experiments have been interpreted in a variety of conflicting fashions. But there does seem to be consensus that there is a significant reduction in annual hours worked by the recipients of payments. (See Burtless and Greenberg, 1983, p. 387, for estimates I believe to be soundly based.)

Numbers of Children and Hours Worked

More children in the family imply lower wealth per person, *ceteris paribus*, and therefore more children imply more work by the parents and by individual children, by the Drive–Effort hypothesis. Data on the matter follow.

(1) In the context of agricultural work by Russian peasants around the turn of this century, Chayanov (1923/1966) showed that a larger number of children (as measured by the ratio of consumers to workers) led to a larger number of workdays, a larger output in roubles, and more land farmed per farmer. From these data I estimated an elasticity of work with respect to the number of consumers as 0.53.[6]

(2) Yotopoulos and Lau (1974) estimated a labour-supply function from Indian data. It is relevant here that their regressions held constant such variables as demand, prices, wage rates, debts, and especially the number of workers in the household. After these factors are allowed for, the elasticity of labour supply with respect to the total number of household family members is a huge 1.12 when their entire model is estimated simultaneously. (The elasticity in a labour-supply regression estimated by itself is 0.67.)

(3) Perhaps the strongest evidence concerning the relationship of dependents to agricultural work per worker comes from Scully's careful study (1962) of 38 Irish farms. He held constant farm size, soil type, costs per acre, and density of livestock, and examined the effect of number of children separately upon (a)

gross output per acre (total money sales), and (b) family income per acre (gross output less costs other than family labour).[7] The results are that an increase of one child (in the mean family with 4.8 children) led to an increase in pounds sterling of $1.133/23.7 = 4.8$ per cent in gross output per acre, and of $0.996/15.2 = 6.5$ per cent in family income per acre. If one assumes that a young child is on the average equal to half an adult consumer-equivalent – certainly on the high side – then a two-parent family with 5.8 rather than 4.8 children has 4.8 rather than 4.4 consumer-equivalents, a difference of $0.5/4.4 = 11$ per cent. The relevant elasticity of work supplied with respect to number of consumers may then be estimated as $(0.048/0.11) = 0.4$ or $(0.065/0.11) = 0.6$.

(4) Smith's (1977, p. 568) previously-mentioned analysis of SEO family data showed that men's work hours are greater by 116 hours per year with each additional child.

(5) Hill (1971, p. 384) found that among the poor white head-of-household respondents to the SEO, more children are associated with considerably more hours worked. For example, having a third child is associated with 219 extra hours of work yearly, a fourth child with 170 extra hours, and a fifth child with 122 extra hours, or about 5, 4, and 3 extra weeks of work a year – large effects indeed.

(6) From survey data of the National Bureau of Economic Research and the Michigan Institute of Social Research, respectively, Landsberger (1971) estimated 0.49 and 2.0 extra weeks of work per child under six. These estimates should be more reliable than Census data.

(7) In Israel's 1971 Survey of Manpower data on hours worked the previous week, Gayer (1974) found that for each additional child, the head of the family worked an extra 149 hours per year, i.e., more than three extra hours per week, an increase of about 7 per cent in work for each child. (It is interesting that the increase in the father's work time is more than three times the decrease in the mother's work time, 42 hours per year per child, so the additional baby apparently increases the total work done.) And in a study of Israeli daily time-budget data, Gronau (1974) found that fathers spend an additional 4 per cent more time working per additional child age 0–5 or 6–12.

(8) Moonlighting is positively and strongly related to number of children (Perella, 1970), as table 5.5 shows.

(9) Shisko and Rostker (1976) found a statistically-significant and economically important effect of family size on propensity to moonlight (elasticity of 0.350) in their multivariate Tobit analysis.

Table 5.5

Number of children	Percentage holding two or more jobs
No children under 18 years	6.0
1 child under 18 years	7.8
2 children under 18 years	8.9
3 or 4 children under 18 years	10.5
5 children under 18 years	11.3

Source: Perella, 1970

One might speculate that the mix of goods that is purchased shifts with family size in such a fashion that the time-intensity rather than the wealth effect explains the larger amount of work done where there are more children. The possibility is raised here only for completeness, however, and not because this is likely to be a major explanation, in my judgement. Also, in addition to the positive effect of children on father's labour-force work, there is a negative effect on mother's labour-force work. But the latter is not relevant here, because our interest is with effort and not with a cost-benefit analysis of children.

Overtime and Wealth

Data on this relationship would be most appropriate and welcome, but I have found none.

Overtime and Number of Children

Ditto.

Saving

Differences in saving behaviour, along with willingness to work, are frequently invoked as an important variable in discussions of differential economic development among countries, between groups within the same country,[8] and in discussions of the decline of nations. Even if physical saving is not a key variable in an advanced society (though this is surely going too far), if the act of saving comes from the same psychological source, with the same causes, as does the exertion of effort, then it may be that a high rate of physical saving in an advanced country could be thought of as a proxy for a more important economic variable – Drive–Effort – rather than as a causal variable in itself. This suggestion is in the same spirit as Kuznets's analyses of institutions and cultures in various countries as being responsible for pairs of variables (or sets of variables) which might otherwise be thought primarily to influence each other.

As analysed by Modigliani and others in a life-cycle framework, lesser wealth leads in a straightforward fashion to a larger rate of physical and financial saving. Interestingly, Becker's analysis of the relationship of wealth to work time discussed earlier is quite parallel.

The act of saving involves the transfer of purchasing power from one present conscious self to some future self with the same identity who will follow the present self. (The view of the person as a set of selves in the present, with other sets of selves to be active in the future, is crucial to making sense of this phenomenon. The classic treatment is that of James (1890/1963, chapter xii).) Such 'giving' from a set of selves in the present to other sets of selves in the future, by way of postponement of consumption, inevitably produces pain, just as does giving to another person; it is sensed as a 'loss' or diminution which – in all except unusual cases of persons who feel relieved of the burden of wealth of any kind when they give it away – is unpleasant. Some drive is required for such an act; experiencing such a drive is one of the elements of what is here called effort.

This view of saving is consistent with the observation that a larger proportion of windfalls is kept for the present selves than is given to future selves. (Transaction and calculation costs might explain why the effect is particularly strong for small windfalls, however.)

This view also is consistent with a larger proportion of each year's income being saved than is saved out of windfalls, if one assumes that much saving is done on a long-term plan and that the self doing the planning at time $t = 0$ is mostly transferring, not from the present sets of selves to future selves, but from specified future sets of selves to other sets of selves even further into the future; analogously, it is easier to distribute wealth or goods fairly between two other persons than between 'oneself' and another person. This also makes sense of Christmas Clubs and other self-forced savings systems; the present self is willing to compel future selves to experience pain, knowing that they (as is the case with the present set of selves) do not like to do so. This accounts for instalment payment plans in which the first payment is deferred; without checking, I'd bet that many Christmas Clubs have the same feature.

It is still necessary to square this view with income-group cross-sectional data, international cross-sections, and historical data. Constancy of the historical saving ratio (in the United States, say), and absence of relationship among countries with different income levels, would be consistent with the idea that the distributions of individuals on this dimension are similar across nations. And lower-income groups could show a lower ratio of saving to income if a lower individual saving ratio (especially with respect to human capital) causes a person to be in a lower income bracket; this would be expected within a population but not across populations. One can therefore explain all types of data consistently and parsimoniously without invoking any psychological propensities that differ by income groups, and without doing much damage to the permanent income hypothesis or to the life-cycle hypothesis. (Behaviour with respect to windfalls is, after all, of minor economic significance, and of interest mostly as a diagnostic device in the study of consumption.)

Saving and Wealth

(1) Patinkin's survey (1965, note M) of studies done up until that time led him to conclude that wealth has a negative effect upon saving.

(2) Mayer's later survey (1972) reached the same conclusion as did Patinkin's review.

(3) Though there is controversy about the size of the effect, all writers apparently agree that wealth in the form of Social Security entitlements has a negative effect upon saving.[9]

(4) Blacks save more than do whites with the same current income.[10] Wealth – measured either as assets or as lifetime income – is likely to be lower for blacks than for whites with the same income, which suggests a negative effect of wealth upon saving.

(5) Using hypothetical questions about saving behaviour under a variety of stipulated conditions, Simon and Barnes (1970) found that saving would be less where wealth was postulated to be higher, and of a magnitude roughly in accord with predictions based on a life-cycle analysis of the stipulated conditions. Shefrin and Thaler (1983) view the deviations from theoretical expectations in the Simon–Barnes study as being consistent with their self-control theory of saving, which has much in common with the view stated above.

Number of Children and Saving

The relationship of saving to the number of children is a matter of controversy (Laumas and Ram, 1982).[11] Theory is ambiguous about the direction in which the relationship may be expected to run. On the one hand, additional children imply lower wealth per person. On the other hand, the time profile of consumption is pushed more towards the present when young adult earners acquire a child, because expenditures on the child will be spread over only (say) the next 15 years, whereas expenditures on the adults will be spread over the next (say) 35 years. This subject has not been well explored analytically, and would seem to be a fruitful topic for study.

Wealth and Aspirations

The higher the economic status of college students in sororities at Berkeley, the lower their 'achievement orientation', as measured by such variables as (a) high grades, and (b) intention of working after graduation (Selvin and Hagstrom, 1963). Working for high grades in school can be interpreted as giving up leisure in order to increase later income. So this result seems a clear-cut negative effect of wealth upon intended effort as measured by achievement orientation.

Length of Unemployment and Reservation Price

The longer a person remains unemployed, the more that assets are depleted, and the poorer the person becomes. It therefore fits the DrEf hypothesis that the asking price for one's labour declines with unemployment, as Kasper (1967) finds in an American questionnaire study, and as Lancaster and Chesher (1983) conclude from two

English questionaire studies. Strengthening this explanation is that a hypothetical increase in the unemployment transfer payment size leads to an increase in the reservation wage (Lancaster and Chesher, 1983). But there are also competing explanations for the phenomenon – downward adjustment in expectations of finding a job, and diminishing marginal utility of leisure (the latter suggested by Kasper).

Testing the Drive–Effort Hypothesis Directly

A variety of data that seem consistent with the Drive–Effort hypothesis have been discussed. Such data may buttress the theoretical argument and increase belief in the hypothesis. But no set of these data constitutes a direct confrontation between theory and data; none provides a test which was constructed for the purpose of trying to falsify the theory at hand. This is not to say that only Popperian falsification matters; in my view, all evidence that is relevant to the subject at hand should reasonably affect one's belief in a theory, rather than belief hanging only on some single formal testing criterion. But one should not stop with an *ad hoc* selection of empirical materials, either.

Two sorts of devices that might provide a rigorous test are as follows. First, one might systematically examine evidence separately on the two links of the chain, running from the Drive–Effort Measure to expended effort, and then from expended effort to economic performance. Though no tests have been set up and carried out specifically to attempt falsifying the theory with respect to these two links, there is at least one systematic study, by Filer (1981), which seems to throw direct light on the latter connection. Filer showed that people with a higher level of what he calls 'drive' – by which he means general activity level – earn higher wages, *ceteris paribus*. And it is reasonable to assume that a higher level of wages is correlated with a higher propensity to accept economic opportunities. Among the personality 'traits' that Filer (1981) studied, 'By far the most important personality trait appears to be general activity, or drive.' This tends to confirm that the theoretical intervening construct used in these chapters not only is observable but also has the hypothesized relationship to the dependent variable, economic output.

For the Drive–Effort hypothesis to be persuasive, there must be a connection between effort and various economic conditions. That is, it must be true that 'Effort is a variable', as Maital (1982, p. 122) puts it. In support of this view, Maital (pp. 126–7) cites evidence showing that the size of the co-operating group has an inverse relationship on the per-person effort expended in group rope-pulling, and on group shouting and clapping.

One might go further and examine systematically whether the Drive–Effort Measure has a (lagged) positive effect upon earnings and entrepreneurial behaviour of individuals and groups, across a sample of nations, or of industries, or both. Wealth might serve as the proxy for the Drive–Effort Measure, which usually is not directly observable. But it would be extremely difficult to construct an after-the-fact study which would deal satisfactorily with the relevant control variables.

Another way to tackle the matter would be with hypothetical questions. In this technique, subjects are asked what they would do under a given set of conditions. The hypothetical conditions are then altered, and the respondent is again asked about his or her behaviour under the new conditions. The difference in people's descriptions of their hypothetical behaviour may then be analysed with respect to the difference in conditions. For example, this technique has been used to estimate demand curves by asking people how much of various goods they think they, or others, would purchase at particular prices (Gilboy, 1931; Shaffer, 1965; Simon, 1965). The technique has also been used to explore the consumption function (Simon and Barnes, 1970). For present purposes, we might specify certain opportunities – say, giving blood for a fee, undertaking a dangerous job, working overtime – under a variety of specified conditions of age, family size, wealth, wages, and so on. Such a test has less appeal for economists than does actual market behaviour. But such a test does have the great virtue of being thoroughly controllable; the comparison between a given respondent's own responses under various conditions holds constant the respondent's demographic, economic, and cultural background, and hence makes easy the sampling requirements. And it is possible to examine whether the differences themselves are influenced by the respondent's background. (They will likely *not* be so influenced under easy assumptions about life-cycle and consumer rationality.)

Animal experiments of the sort carried out with apes and slot machines might also test this theory well, and especially the shape of the Drive–Effort Measure with respect to wealth. For example, one could vary the ape's stock of tokens and observe the amount of effort the ape will expend to 'earn' additional tokens in a given period of time. One could also vary the 'purchasing power' of the tokens to see how effort is affected. I have not found any work of this sort done heretofore, however.

Concluding Remarks

The aforegoing data, taken together, would seem to demonstrate that there is an inverse relationship between wealth and work effort, as the Drive–Effort hypothesis suggests. Evidence has not been presented showing that the second element of the Drive–Effort Measure, a larger pay-off, induces more effort, *ceteris paribus*, but this proposition would not seem to require any demonstration. Together, these elements support the view that more effort will be produced when the Drive–Effort Measure is higher. No evidence has been provided here on the specific shape of the function; that will have to wait for further study. But the specific shape is not crucial in the applications discussed here.

Notes

1 'Great Productivity at a Utah Coal Mine is Called "God's Plan"', *Wall Street Journal*, 12 April 1984, p. 1.
2 'Ohio Firm Relies on Incentive-Pay System to Motivate Workers and Maintain Profits', *Wall Street Journal*, 12 August 1983, p. 15.
3 'Back to Piecework: More Companies Want to Base Pay Increases on the Output of Their Employees', *Wall Street Journal*, 15 November 1985, p. 15.
4 Much of this section is drawn from Simon (1966).
5 Income per person, the variable used in all the studies mentioned in this section, is an excellent proxy for wealth in a long-run group average context. With respect to consumer-held wealth in housing and other physical assets, lifetime income is on average a good measure of total wealth, and holdings of consumer assets are surely adjusted to lifetime

income by households. With respect to producer wealth, the relative invariance in the capital-output ratio across nations and time-periods enables us to work backwards from income (output) to wealth (though recognizing all the defects in national estimates of capital, such as farmland evaluation).

6 For a summary of this material, see Simon (1977), pp. 189–92.
7 On only nine of the farms were there children of ages where they contributed any work at all to the farm, and hence the number of workers 'has had little influence on the results of the analysis' (Scully, 1962, p. 121).
8 For further reading see: Myrdal (1968); and Nair (1962).
9 For example, see Feldstein (1974), pp. 905–26.
10 For references, see Simon and Simon (1968); and Hodges (1982).
11 For a general earlier summary, see Simon (1977), chapter 10. See also the negative effect of children on saving found by Smith (1977). Concerning the continuing controversy about the cross-national relationship see Leff (1980); Billsborrow (1980); and Ram (1982; 1984).

6

Illustration: The Effect of
Competition upon Effort

The economic role of competition is to discipline the various
participants in economic life to provide their goods and services
skillfully and cheaply . . . When one asks . . . whether the
competition of three merchants will serve better than
two . . . the answers prove to be elusive.
George Stigler (1968, p. 181)

Introduction

Does the discipline of additional competitors lead to greater competitive effort and better service? This chapter offers an analysis to
answer the question. And surprisingly, it is found that there are at
least some circumstances where the answer does not coincide with
our professional intuition, though in most circumstances the analysis
confirms that more total effort will be expended by two competitors
than by one.

It is worth recalling that the effect of competition is not a settled
matter even with respect to price. There are various conjectures,
going back to Cournot (1838/1963), about mechanisms that lead to a
duopoly price lower than a monopoly price, and the conclusion is then
simply extrapolated to triopoly and beyond, without formal argument.
But even in the monopoly–duopoly price comparison, a good many
assumptions must be made before one can even be sure theoretically

that the duopolists will not settle at the monopoly price,[1] and these assumptions are often not appropriate.

With respect to other competitive behaviour, there exists even less economic explanation of how and why two or three competitors will serve the public differently than will one firm alone – if they do. Economists *believe* that service will be better if there are three restaurants or airlines than if there is only one. Certainly there is lots of casual evidence that competition improves service. The competition of Hertz and Avis is a legendary example; Macy's versus Gimbels is another. The usual explanation offered is that competitors are forced to try harder – that is, to exert more effort – than is a monopolist who supposedly can enjoy the 'quiet life' that Hicks (1935/1952, p. 369) said is the best of all monopoly profits. But this explanation is far less precise than the sort of explanation economists are accustomed to accept. By analogy, one could say about price, too, that it is expected to be lower in duopoly than in monopoly because competitors will 'try harder', and let it go at that; such an answer would be beneath professional contempt, however.

The aim of this chapter is to construct an apparatus that will provide a reasonably systematic analysis of some non-price behaviour in monopoly compared to duopoly. The analysis applies to individuals and business organizations which are assumed to differ in their human and economic characteristics (including their wealth), rather than where the organizations are conceived of as identical machines.[2]

Effort need not be measured directly in this conceptual framework, any more than such intervening variables as utility or risk preference need to be measured directly in the economic analyses in which they are commonly used. But if one did wish to measure effort directly, it is certainly measurable in a variety of ways, for example, objectively by the number of smiles exhibited, the sound level of ragslaps by a bootblack, or subjectively on a self-rating scale, even if it cannot be measured as simply as can money or time inputs. The logic underlying measurement of a similar concept that is commonly thought to be more difficult to measure interpersonally – utility – is discussed elsewhere – Simon (1974).

Considered first is the impact of an additional (second) competitor in a given market, as compared with the situation where just one 'firm' is operating. This is the comparison which economists seem to have in mind when contrasting monopoly with duopoly. The number of competitors allowed is assumed to be regulated (by law or otherwise) independently of the competitors' actions, and hence the effects of firms' behaviour upon prospective entry need not be considered.

Considered next is another prototypical comparison: two artificially-separated identical markets each with a single competitor, versus the same two no-longer-separated markets with the barriers removed so that both firms compete for all of the combined market.

The geometrical analysis is crude and numerical, and will require a good many steps. The reason for this laborious and inelegant presentation is that the concepts being worked with here are deceptively slippery, and experience shows it necessary to nail down their interpretations in great detail if confusion is to be avoided. Hence I hope that the reader will bear with me and not be put off by this plodding prolix approach. A more elegant proof using the calculus will appear elsewhere (Simon and Rashid, 1986).

Eventually the central idea in this chapter should link up with the rapidly burgeoning literature on industrial structure.[3] But though that body of work includes advertising and modes of competition other than price in its research programme, it has so far concentrated upon price. And the outcome of the analysis for non-price competition is quite different than for price competition, as this chapter shows, and as may also be seen elsewhere.[4] The work on this chapter also has an intellectual link to Leibenstein's X-efficiency and to the 'slack' concept, slack being the opposite side of the coin from effort.

Elements of the Analysis

Imagine a bootblack A having the sole right to operate in a large office building. (We will shortly imagine a second bootblack B also given the right to operate in the same place.) Assuming price fixed and no paid advertising, the owner-operator bootblack's own services are the only significant input. Therefore 'profit' (which equals sales revenue in this case) depends only upon effort. Effort is the amount of energy A

puts into snapping the rag, the amount of warmth in A's smile, and other activities which affect consumer reaction. The number of clients that A serves during the eight hours the building is open depends only upon the amount of effort. When not actually shining shoes, A waits for clients and loafs, so time is not a variable input in this case.

Figure 6.1 (similar to figure 4.1) shows the Incremental Drive–Effort (IncDrEf) function which portrays the additional effort that A is *willing to expend* at various levels of wealth in hand in order to obtain an additional dollar of revenue, at two levels of initial wealth. The declining convex function indicates that the more assets A has in hand at any given moment, the larger the increment of revenue that would be required to induce him or her to exert an additional unit of effort.

The IncDrEf function is hypothesized to have the form

$$
\begin{aligned}
\text{IncDrEf} &= a\left(\frac{W_{n+1} - W_n}{W_n}\right) \\
&= a\left(\frac{\text{Incremental payoff}}{\text{Wealth in hand at decision moment}}\right) \quad (6.1)
\end{aligned}
$$

where W_n is the wealth prior to undertaking the incremental opportunity, and W_{n+1} is the expected wealth after the incremental effort is exerted. In other guises, this function has a long theoretical history, and it seems to fit the results of various psychological experiments. But though *some* shape must be chosen for illustrative purposes, *the exact shape of the function has absolutely no bearing upon the argument given here*; the only requirement is that the incremental effort function be monotonically decreasing with wealth in hand.

Wealth would usually be defined as present assets plus future lifetime earnings contingent on some prior set of decisions. But in the present case, where the situation studied is sufficiently simple that the decisions about the present day's effort and opportunities can be considered independent of all similar future decisions, and where the day's income can be considered small relative to present assets, one can for convenience consider only the existing assets as wealth. (One might think of this day as the last working day in A's life.)

Becker's analysis of the allocation of time yields the proposition that, under plausible assumptions, an increase in wealth leads to a

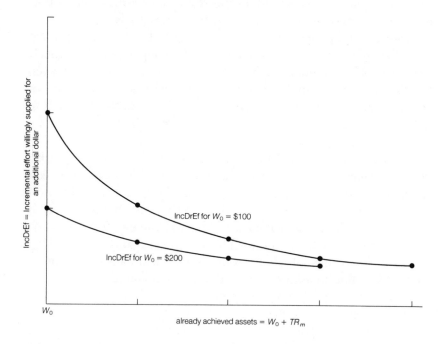

Figure 6.1 The relationship of incremental Drive–Effort to opportunity and wealth

$$\textit{Principle of construction: IncDrEF} = \frac{(TR_{m+1} + W_0) - (TR_m + W_0)}{(TR_m + W_0)}$$

where TR_m = total revenue obtained from efforts until now

TR_{m+1} = total revenue from efforts until now plus another unit of effort

W_0 = initial endowment

IncDrEf = effort willingly supplied for another dollar

decrease in the amount of time that the person would spend on work. This implies a function that has the same declining characteristics as does the Incremental Drive–Effort function in figure 6.1. Therefore, as long as the analysis does not depend upon the specific exponential form, one may broaden the effort concept to include time and managerial attention as well as other effort. One may then either regard the function as referring to effort alone, or to time alone, or to both. This may be reassuring to the reader concerned about effort being too evanescent a concept for economic analysis.

More generally, the analysis fits any output that has an increasing cost of supply with increasing quantities of the input. But this is likely to be true only of inputs which are limited to the resources of a given individual. Other inputs can ordinarily be purchased at constant or declining prices as volume increases, and plant size can be chosen so that larger quantities can be supplied at a cost that is at least not increasing if not actually declining.

Calculating the Drive–Effort function should be done marginally, in accordance with the facts about how the decision-maker sequentially arrives at the decision. The bootblack first inquires whether a first unit of effort should be expended. If the answer is 'yes', then inquiry is made about an additional unit of effort, and so on until the answer is 'no'. The wealth in each calculation ($W_o + TR_m$) includes the results of all decisions up to that point. This is in contradistinction to asking about various *total* amounts of effort; this latter procedure would only be appropriate for an opportunity which must be accepted or rejected as a whole, on a take-it-or-leave-it basis, rather than for an opportunity where one is able to choose whichever amount of effort one wishes. Further discussion of the creation of the IncDrEf function is in the appendix to this chapter.

Next the *effects* of effort upon sales must be brought into the analysis. To explicate as clearly as possible, this relationship will be portrayed in several ways. To begin, figure 6.2 shows the volume of sales that will be produced by various amounts of effort. The solid line shows the cumulative sales response (*TR*) at various effort levels, and the dotted line shows the incremental sales response per unit of effort (*MR*) at successive effort levels. This figure is similar to the graph of an advertising-to-sales relationship, which can be seen as a special case of the effort–sales relationship. The *TR* curve is drawn concave, just as the revenue function is concave with respect to advertising.[5] The *TR* function cuts the vertical axis above the origin because the bootblack will get some business even if he/she makes no effort at all to do so, but instead simply 'provides the basic goods', i.e., shines the shoes mechanically with no flourish or conversation, and without making his/her kiosk bright and attractive. From this is calculated the marginal sales response function (*MR*).

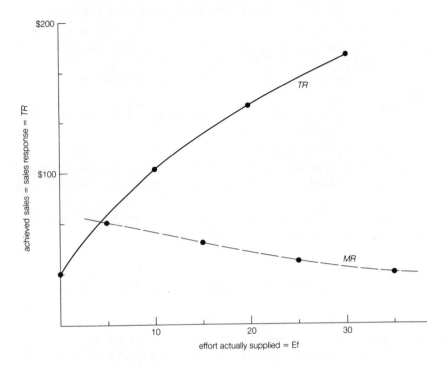

Figure 6.2 The relationship of sales response to effort exerted
Principles of construction:

$(TR \mid \text{Ef} = 10) = \$100$

$(TR \mid \text{Ef} = 20) - (TR \mid \text{Ef} = 10) = 0.8 \times \$100$

$(TR \mid \text{Ef} = 30) - (TR \mid \text{Ef} = 20) = 0.8 \times 0.8 \times \$100$

etcetera

$$MR \text{ at Ef} = 15 \approx \frac{(TR \mid \text{Ef} = 10) - (TR \mid \text{Ef} = 0)}{10}$$

$$MR \text{ at Ef} = 15 \approx \frac{(TR \mid \text{Ef} = 20) - (TR \mid \text{Ef} = 10)}{10}$$

etcetera

Note: *MR* is multiplied by 10 to make the figure more readable.

Now one can determine the amount of effort that will be chosen by *A* under existing circumstances. The marginal data in figure 6.2 are first mapped into the form of figure 6.3, where the *MR* relationship is shown by what may now be called the Incremental *Necessary* Effort

(IncNecEf) line, that is, the additional effort required at each level of sales to obtain an additional dollar of sales. IncNecEf is the transformation of the marginal relationship derived from the cumulative effort–sales relationship (TR) shown in figure 6.2.

Also shown in figure 6.3 is an IncDrEf function redrawn from figure 6.1.

The point of intersection Z of the IncNecEf and IncDrEf functions in figure 6.3 determines the amount of effort that A will expend. Up until point Z, the required effort for an additional dollar of sales (Incremental Necessary Effort, or IncNecEf) has been less than the effort that A would be willing to expend (IncDrEf) to obtain an additional dollar; at effort levels above Z, the opposite is true.

The difference between the IncNecEf and the IncDrEf is similar to producer surplus in conventional analysis.

One Versus Two Competitors in the Same Market

Now a second competitor B is added to the same building. The cumulative sales response (TR) function in figure 6.2 may be understood as the sales that will result from various amounts of *total* effort in the market, that is, the sum of the efforts by A and B (or by A alone when A is a monopolist).

Proposition 1: In a given market with two competitors rather than a monopolist, there will be less effort exerted per firm, but greater total effort

To bring out the nature of the process most clearly, let us shift temporarily to the case in which TR goes through the origin – that is, where no sales are made without some effort. On this assumption, figure 6.4 shows the monopolist's function, as well as A's function computed for two levels of effort by B. (Zero effort by B would in this case lead to a function for A identical to the monopolist's function.) The amount of sales obtained by each competitor is assumed proportional to the effort exerted by that firm relative to the sum of the effort by the two, and the total sales by the two are equal to the sales that would be obtained by a monopolist exerting that much effort.

IncNecEf functions calculated in rough increments from figure 6.4

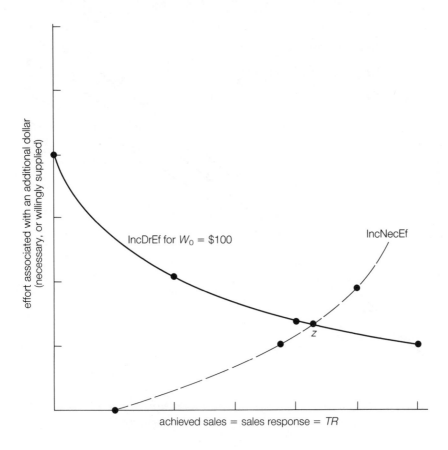

*Figure 6.3 Analysis for deciding whether to supply effort in a given case
Principle of construction: IncDrEf$_{\$100}^{A}$ from figure 6.1; IncNecEf from MR
in figure 6.2*

are shown in figure 6.5. There one sees that the IncNecEf functions for A are higher than for the monopolist, because the slopes of competitor A's *TR* functions in figure 6.4 are lower at each effort level than are the monopolist's, and A will therefore exert *less effort* in a competitively divided market than he or she will as a monopolist in the same market. This can be seen even for the case in which A's IncNecEf effort function would be perfectly horizontal (as is the function for the incremental cost of advertising, aside from discounts), no matter what its height.

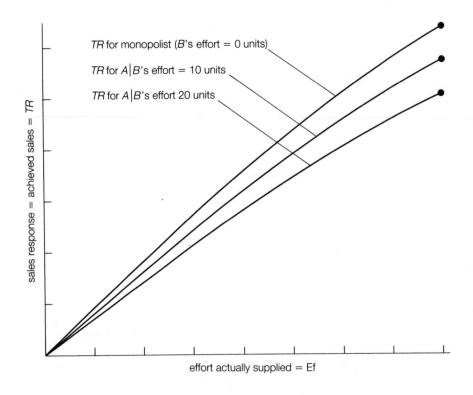

Figure 6.4 Total revenue for monopolist with TR *through origin and for competitor*
A (*given difference levels of effort by competitor* B)

The *total* effort exerted by the two competitors *A* and *B* together,
however, is *greater* than would be exerted by a monopolist alone, and
in that sense the public is better served; this total effort is the central
issue which this chapter addresses. Ultimately one wants a neat
formal proof of this proposition, but the following argument should
suffice to make the point for now: the intersections of *A*'s IncNecEf
function with the IncDrEf function are at more than the effort
levels of the monopolist's intersection, and hence two competitors'
efforts add to more than the monopolist's. Furthermore, it is rather
obvious that this would even be so if the IncDrEf function were
horizontal.

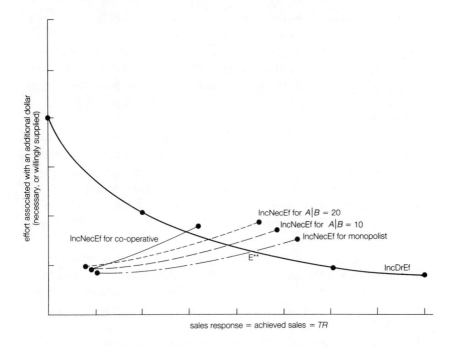

Figure 6.5   Decision-making for A *given various levels of effort by competitor* B

Principle of construction: IncNecEf^{monop}, IncNecEf$^{A|B=10}$ and IncNecEf$^{A|B=20}$
from figure 6.4. IncNecEf$^{co-operative}$ represents IncNecEf^A taken from the TR^{monop}
function in figure 6.4 in this fashion:
*IncNecEf^A = 1/2(IncNecEf^{monop}) at 1/2 (*TR$^{monop}|DrEf$)
Note: The IncNecEf functions have been quadrupled to clarify the figure. Figure 6.5
is a transformation of figures 6.4 and 6.1

Corollary (a): The proposition holds even if the competitors
co-operate to the utmost

To make the argument more conclusive, consider the 'co-operative'
function in figure 6.5, representing *A*'s effort and sales results on the
assumption that *A* and *B* always exert the same amount of effort
(which they would do only if they have the same IncDrEf functions).
Furthermore, consider how things would be if the IncDrEf function

were horizontal, as it would be for advertising. If so, and if the competitors exerted (and planned to exert) the same amount of effort (or advertising) as each other, they would expend just as much effort (or spend just as much for advertising) in total as would a monopolist. It would then be as if they were each half-shareholders in the monopolist; they would be moving up the same *TR* function as the monopolist, with the same objectively-caused stopping point.

With a function for *A* where *B*'s effort is instead assumed fixed at any particular level, *A*'s IncNecEf function lies below the co-operative function, as seen in figure 6.5. The reason is that with any increase in *A*'s effort in the co-operative function, something 'bad' (an increase in *B*'s effort) is assumed to happen along with the 'good' result of an increase in sales to *A*, when *A* exerts an additional unit of effort. This 'bad' does not occur in functions where *B*'s effort is fixed and hence *A* will exert more effort with the latter. And this proves that *A* will exert more than half the effort of a monopolist, and hence competition produces more total effort, even with a horizontal DrEf function. (One might imagine some perverse functions that would induce less effort than the 'co-operative' function, but these implausibilities need not be considered here.)

Furthermore, since the IncDrEf function is sloped downwards rather than being horizontal, the distance between the cutting points on the monopolist's and the competitors' *MR* function is less than with a horizontal line, and the co-operative function then produces more than half the effort of the monopolist's function. *A fortiori*, then, the two competitors' efforts add to more than a monopolist's effort. Also, the amount of total effort per dollar of sales is obviously greater with two competitors than with the monopolist.

It is illuminating that the concavity of the response function and the convexity of the IncDrEf function are *both* needed to produce the result that competition leads to more effort in the 'co-operative' case. If the IncDrEf function were horizontal, total effort in that case would be no more than in monopoly. But if their IncDrEf functions are convex, this will not be true for the co-operative function; the competitors will be 'poorer' than the monopolist, and hence will exert more effort than 'half' a monopolist.

Now let us analyse this case in a more rigorous fashion, which also brings out the driving mechanism more clearly. Consider that the monopolist's chosen equilibrium is where

$$\frac{d(\text{IncDrEf})}{d(TR)} = \frac{(\text{IncNecEf})}{d(TR)} \tag{6.2}$$

which is at the effort level E^{**}, as seen in figure 6.5. Now assume that an additional competitor enters the same market, and that the chosen effort levels for firms A and B are $\hat{E}_A$ and $\hat{E}_B$. Suppose that the level of total effort remains the same, that is $E_A + \hat{E}_B = E^{**}$. If so, at least one of E_A and E_B must be less than E^{**}, say $\hat{E}_A$. If so,

$$\left(\frac{d(\text{IncDrEf})}{d(TR)}|\hat{E}_A\right) > \left(\frac{d(\text{IncDrEf})}{d(TR)}|\text{E}^{**}\right) \tag{6.3}$$

because A's effort is less than the monopolist's; and A is therefore further back toward the origin, and therefore higher, on the IncDrEf function in figure 6.5. But now one notices that, on the assumption that $\hat{E}_B$ is fixed, the return to additional effort by A would be the same as it would for the monopolist at E^{**}. (That is, if $\hat{E}_B$ is fixed, and $\hat{E}_A + \hat{E}_B = E^{**}$, the A's response function IncNecEf at $\hat{E}$ would be the same as IncNecEf for the monopolist at E^{**}.) If so,

$$\left(\frac{d(\text{IncDrEf})}{d(TR)}|\hat{E}_A\right) > \left(\frac{d(\text{IncNecEf})}{d(TR)}|E_A\right) = \left(\frac{d(\text{IncNecEf})}{d(TR)}|E^{**}\right) \tag{6.4}$$

That is, A would then not be in an equilibrium at $\hat{E}_A$, and would exert additional effort. (In other words, A at $\hat{E}_A$ would get the same return from a unit of additional effort as would the monopolist at E^{**}, but would 'value' it more because of being at a higher level of willingness to exert effort to gain an additional unit of revenue, due to having less wealth.) This is also true for B. Hence

$$(E_A^* + E_B^*) > E^{**}, \text{ where } E_A^* > \hat{E}_A$$

by the argument just given.

It has been shown that the total effort expended by A and B will exceed that of a monopolist in the same market (assuming all have the same IncDrEf functions). But the increase in effort expended arises from a single simple cause: The existence of competitor B makes A poorer – that is, he or she has less wealth – than a monopolist when the total effort expended (and pay-offs obtained) by A and B are equal to those of a monopolist, and therefore either or both of them has greater willingness than the monopolist to exert additional effort at that point.

It should be noted that the result obtained does not depend upon concavity of the *TR* function; it would hold even if *TR* were linear.

The case in which the competitors' IncDrEf functions differ has not yet been analysed. But I doubt that the results will differ from those discussed above.

One may wonder how allowing for more fully interactive competition would affect the results. A long-run multi-period dynamic analysis, bringing in many of the relevant competitive considerations, would be much more complex. And there will not be any one single determinate result; this one can conclude with surety from the Simon–Ben-Ur (1981) analysis of duopolistic competition in advertising, as well as from the similar Simon–Puig–Aschoff (1973) analysis of price competition. Even in the case of advertising competition, where (unlike the situation in which the competitive variable is the amount of effort) there can be no difference with respect to the cost of inputs (that is, where the counterpart of the IncDrEf function is the same for both firms), the outcome differs depending upon initial conditions, the discount factor, probabilistic assessments of the competitor's behaviour, etc. With the additional complication of differences in IncDrEf functions, the range of indeterminacy must be even greater.

Interactive competition is not really important in this context, however. The analysis at hand involves only the ex post effort positions of the competitors, and it does not matter by what gaming process they arrive at those positions. The discussion so far has dealt with the optimizing position for *A*, given some level of effort by *B*, which could be assumed to be the optimizing effort level for *B* given the effort level by *A*. There could be more than one set of mutually-optimizing positions, though the analysis has not yet reached that far. But the conclusions reached above seem to hold for each pair of competitive-outcome positions, no matter how arrived at, and that is all that seems to matter for now.

Corollary (b): The proposition holds whether the market TR *function does or does not pass through the origin*

Returning to a market in which the monopolist's *TR* cuts the vertical axis *above* the origin (figure 6.6), one sees that all the conclusions drawn for the through-the-origin function hold, *a fortiori*, because the *TR* functions are steeper for *A* in the above-the-origin case than in the through-the-origin case, whereas the monopolist's function has the same slope at all effort points for both cases. This conclusion can be seen in a rough way by comparing the two figures visually. It also follows from the fact that *A*'s function passes through the origin at even the slightest effort by *B* – say 0.00001 of a unit of effort – but at positive effort by *A*, the function then rises almost to what it would have been if *B* exerted zero effort, in which case *A*'s function is the same as the monopolist's function. Hence *A*'s function must be steeper in the early range than the monopolist's function, while it has almost the same slope in the later range; in comparison, at 0.00001 units of effort by *B* in the through-the-origin case, *A*'s function would be the same as the monopolist's throughout. Even in the absence of a general proof, this should satisfy the reader that the conclusions drawn from the through-the-origin case apply to the above-the-origin case.

As suggested earlier, advertising can be seen as a special case of the analysis given here, in which the input cost function is linear and horizontal (a given amount of advertising space or time costs almost the same no matter how much you advertise), and is the same for both competitors (who therefore will advertise the same amounts under such simple conditions), whereas the IncDrEf function is not likely to be constant, and may differ for the two competitors. Therefore, if the monopolist's *TR* function with respect to advertising passes through the origin, competitors will advertise the same amount in total as will a monopolist, on the same reasoning given above in discussion of a 'co-operative' *TR*-effort function with a horizontal effort curve.[6] Otherwise, the conclusions drawn above are consistent with the results if the concept of effort is replaced by the concept of advertising.[7]

This general line of analysis enables us to determine the effect of one competitor's wealth, and his/her consequent willingness to exert effort, upon the other competitor's actual effort. The greater the wealth of *B*, the less effort *B* is willing to exert, and the higher and steeper will be *A*'s response function. Hence *A* will exert more effort if *B* is wealthier and exerts less effort. This is the opposite of the effect that one expects in sports competition where greater effort by

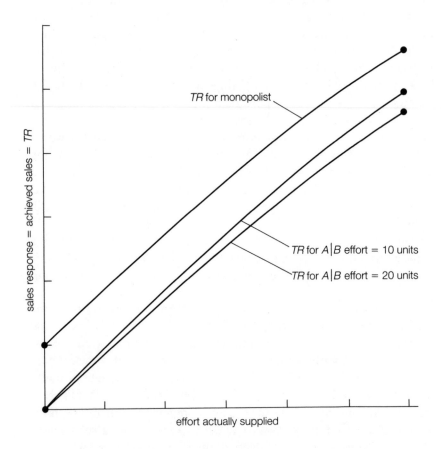

Figure 6.6 Total revenue for monopolist not through origin
Principles of construction: $\mathrm{TR}^{monop} = (5 + \mathrm{TR}^{monop}$ *in figure 6.5);*
$(\mathrm{TR}^{A} \mid DrEf^{B} = 10) =$ *same principle as in figure 6.4*

one competitor is thought to induce greater effort by the others, under most circumstances (but not if the greater effort by one dispirits the others). There may also be a sport-like competitive effect in business, perhaps opposing the effect analysed here, and perhaps even dominating this one empirically. But that phenomenon would require a very different sort of theoretical analysis.

One may wonder about the social effects of there being more competitors who expend more effort in total but less per competitor. The public gains by the greater effort, but might lose through the lessened output per competitor. This is exactly the common argument against allowing an unlimited number of taxi cabs on the streets of New York, or shops in the bazaar of an Indian city, or bag-hustlers outside a poor country's airport. Presumably, however, each of the competitors in such a situation could not be more productively employed elsewhere in the economy, or else he/she would move into other situations. So a general-equilibrium analysis gives no reason to worry about this effect. Furthermore, if the firms under discussion are larger than a single operator, and if the Drive–Effort effect seeps through to the employees as it affects the owners, there will be only public gain. There will be no social loss from diminished time input, because the number of employees would be appropriately smaller in competitive firms than in a monopolist firm.

One Versus Two Competitors in a Duopoly Market Twice the Size of the Monopoly Market

Imagine now two contiguous identical market areas – two towns, or two entry corridors of an office building – which are separated by fiat. Each of two firms has a licence to operate in each separated market, and is forbidden to compete in the other's market. Let us compare such a situation with that in which the barrier to competition between the two markets is removed, and both firms (but only these two firms) are then permitted to compete in both the contiguous markets. The combined market is simply twice as large as each original uncombined market. For specificity one may think about two bootblacks A and B operating in the separated corridors of an office building, again assuming price fixed and no advertising.

We shall also assume no economies of scale in effort. More specifically, if the TR function in a separate market yields S sales at E effort, in the merged market a total effort of $2E$ yields $2S$ total sales.

Unlike the divided-market analysis discussed earlier, the conclusion differs depending upon the conditions of competition.

Let us first examine the case where the TR function cuts the vertical axis above the origin. Figure 6.7 shows the *TR* function for the combined market, that is, the sales response to the sum of the two competitors' efforts.

Proposition 2: If competitors in merged markets co-operate fully, they will exert no more effort than when each operates as a monopolist in a separate single market

If *A* and *B* decide on effort levels co-operatively, they will produce the same amounts of effort in total as they would when operating as monopolists in separated markets. The explanation is that their wealth levels would also be the same at those points in both cases.

That is, in figure 6.7 the curve marked 'co-operative *TR*' shows the response either to a monopolist in a separate market, or to one competitor in the combined market assuming the other competitor exerts equal effort. This result is sharply at variance with the divided-market case, where co-operation among two competitors leads to larger total effort than a monopolist exerts, because the two competitors are 'poorer' than a single monopolist in the same market. It was pointed out in the divided-market co-operative case that the result of greater effort depends upon both concavity in the *TR* function and curvature in the IncDrEf function. In the merged-markets case, the curvature in the IncDrEf function has no differential effect because the function is effectively the same for firms as co-operating competitors and as monopolists. (The above discussion assumes the same IncDrEf functions for the two competitors. Differences in the function are explored in a richer context below.)

The outcome that the two firms may reach a co-operative outcome which is no better for the public than a monopolist in the merged markets resembles the situation in price competition. But in competition with effort (as with advertising) there is less incentive for each competitor to cheat on a co-operative agreement than there is with price, because an across-the-board price reduction (the sort usually discussed) affects all customers and not just the marginal customers, whereas a change in effort only works at the margin.[8] Additionally, price cuts can be secret, whereas competition with effort or advertising is revealed publicly. Therefore, the potential benefits of competition with effort or advertising are more likely to be

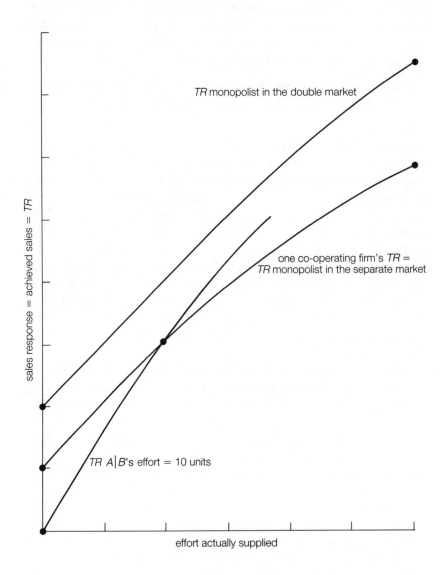

Figure 6.7 Two separated markets compared to the two markets combined into one
Principle of construction: for the merged markets, double each effort level for the
monopolist in figure 6.6, and double the sales results. For A in the presence of B
exerting DrEf^B = 10 units of effort, for each level of A's effort find the results for
the monopolist at (DrEf^A + 10), and attribute to A sales in the same proportion as
A's effort

frustrated by agreement among the competitors, explicit or implicit, than in price competition. For example, competing stores are more likely to cut prices surreptitiously or with various gimmicks than they are to sneak a little bit later closing time.

Proposition 3: If the firms do not co-operate, there will be more total effort when markets are merged than when separate

Unlike the single firm's *TR* function in the co-operative situation when the *TR* function does not go through the origin, the function for *A* with a *fixed* effort by *B* goes through the origin, and then rises more steeply than the combined function crossing it at the point where *A*'s effort is equal to *B*'s. Because the slope is greater, and marginal response is greater, the marginal function must cross the IncDrEf function at a higher level of effort for *A* than when in a separate market. For example, assume that in a separated market, where sales are greater than zero at zero effort, *A*'s optimum effort is DrEf* = 10 units. With the two markets combined, if *A* and *B* each exert ten units of effort, *A* will get the same response as in the separated market. But with *B*'s effort fixed at 10 units, the marginal response to *A*'s effort is greater at DrEf = 10 units in the combined markets than in the separate market.

To prove this rigorously, let us first recall our assumption about the distribution of sales among the competitors: of the sales resulting from the total effort exerted by the two competitors, each competitor receives sales in the same proportion as its effort is to the total. By analogy, two persons putting fishing lines into a lake at random places will catch fish in proportion to other numbers of lines, while the total catch is a concave-downward function of the total number of lines.

To continue the analysis in this analogy: imagine a rectangular pond divided into two halves by a fish-proof barrier. Each half is fished by a monopolist. Consider simply one day's fishing, without worrying about depletion effects in the future, and assume that each person fishing has the same Drive–Effort function. Each person puts in lines until the marginal return from an additional line equals the marginal Drive–Effort from putting in an additional line.

Now imagine that the barrier is removed. If the two fisherpersons collaborate as a firm, they would put in the same total number of lines as they did when separate monopolists, as discussed above.

Now imagine that they do not act co-operatively. If *A* assumes that

B will put in as many lines as B did as a separate monopolist, which is half the number of lines they would put in as a joint firm, A will now reason as follows: If I put in one additional line, the return to that line will be greater than if both of us put in additional lines, because the probability of getting a catch on one of two additional lines is less than the probability of getting a catch on just one additional line due to there being fewer total lines in the pond in the latter case. Therefore, if earlier I was indifferent about putting in an additional line conditional on B also putting one in, I will no longer be indifferent about putting in an additional line when I assume B does not. Therefore, A's imagined response function is different than either the function for the joint firm or for the separate-market monopolists. The geometry implies more effort for A, and hence more total effort, when the two are not co-operating than when A and B are operating separately or when they are co-operating.[9]

Now what about when B's effort is above or below DrEf*, A's chosen level of effort in the separated market? The conclusion is not so straightforward or conclusive. First, ask *why* B might be above or below DrEf. The simplest assumption is that B has the same IncDrEf function as does A but decides – and signals so to A – that he will exert effort greater than DrEf* simply because of miscalculation or other random influence. If A now optimizes, its decline in effort below DrEf* will be less than the increment that B is above it because of the slopes of the IncNecEf function above and below DrEf*; the sum of efforts by A and B will then be greater than in separated markets. For example, if both A and B would optimize at DrEf* = 10, but B exerts 20 units of effort by mistake, A would optimize by dropping effort about 6 units if the IncNecEf function were horizontal, and therefore would reduce effort by even less than 6 units because IncNecEf is upward-sloped instead of horizontal. On the other hand, if B is below DrEf* by random occurrence, then A will move less far above DrEf* than B is below it, by the same reasoning, and the total effort exerted will be *less* than in separate markets. However, after B discovers the miscalculation, he/she will move somewhat toward DrEf* (but not all the way to it) as long as A is above DrEf*. But then A would move toward DrEf*, there would be iterations, and they would then both end up near DrEf*.

If A and B have different IncDrEf functions, the matter is even more complex. Assume that B's IncDrEf function leads to less effort than does A's. B will then exert effort above DrEf*, but not as much as B is below it. But the difference between DrEf* and B's effort is not all due to competition, but rather some of the difference is due to B's IncDrEf function. Here is one scenario of what might happen.

Assume A plans effort DrEf* and B plans effort $(1/a)$DrEf* where $a > 1$, because B is wealthier than A. They meet and tell their true plans. They then calculate new optimizing points, both responding to the difference [DrEf* − $(1/a)$DrEf*]. B moves back on his/her DrEf − that is, upwards − and also up the marginal response function, both of which buffer each successive reduced unit of effort more strongly. A moves down his/her DrEf function toward more effort, and also down the marginal response function, both of which buffer each additional unit of effort more strongly. Which competitor would move further in response to the gap, i.e., whether B's reduction in effort would be greater or less than A's increase in effort, may depend upon the particular shape of the TR function. And there would then be subsequent adjustments. But it is probable that each of the adjustments would have the same direction of effect as the first one.

(The tell-the-truth sort of interactive process discussed here, without gaming, might serve very well as a simple model of the non-price interactive process, in contrast to the analytic needs in a price-adjustment process. The comments made earlier about the possibility of creating a dynamic model of interactive competition apply here as well as to the one-market case.)

Proposition 4: If the TR function goes through the origin, there will be more effort expended by two firms competing in a merged market than when they are monopolists in separate markets, but the effect will not be as marked as when the function does not pass through the origin

This proposition may be seen intuitively in the geometry of the two cases.

Discussion

(1) The results obtained for the merged-market case are in no way dependent upon the shape of the Drive−Effort function, nor even on it being a declining function. Therefore, the result immediately

generalizes to advertising, for which the cost function corresponding to the effort function is flat. In the divided-market case, the driving force is the effort function, because there is a difference in the wealths of monopolists and competitors. But there is no such wealth difference between competitor and monopolist in the merged-market case. Rather, the moving force is the change in opportunity between the separate-market and the merged-market cases.

Therefore, together the two cases illustrate the operation of both blades of the Drive–Effort function's scissors – the effort scissor in the divided-market case, and the wealth scissor in the merged-market case.

(2) Absent from this discussion of effort exerted in competition is the sense of struggle to outdo the competition before he/she outdoes you. This is the feeling of the heat of battle, to be compared to the monopolist's quiet life. Upon reflection, it seems that the operational counterpart of this phenomenon is founded in expectations about the competitor's behaviour, with actions taken contingent in these other expectations. This interaction can only be comprehended systematically with a rich simulation model, such as Simon, Puig, and Aschoff (1973) or Simon and Ben-Ur (1982). But though the subjective reflection of these activities may be the most noticeable aspect of the competition, that element is of relevance to psychologists rather than to economists.

(3) The effects of market structure upon the adoption of innovation illustrate the Drive–Effort hypothesis. Primeaux's work (1977) on competitive electric monopolies shows that competition-induced effort reduces cost by about 10 per cent of average cost, though adoption of innovations is not separated from other managerial efforts in that analysis.

Cases of adoption of innovations that have no cost *except* the effort of making the change (and perhaps a relatively tiny expenditure of time) should be particularly relevant. For example, a historical examination of the adoption of the now-universal 'January White Sale' of linens by department stores (Simon and Golembo, 1967) showed that stores in small towns were much slower than were stores in big cities to adopt the practice, though there was no installation cost and the practice quickly proved profitable (as shown by continued use by almost all stores after initial use). The only likely explanation is the stronger lash of competition in large cities, which fits with the analysis of monopoly-duopoly effort offered above.

Summary and Conclusions

The central question addressed in this chapter is the amount of total effort that will be expended if there are two competitors in a market rather than one. The core of the analysis is the hypothesized relationship between (a) wealth, and (b) the effort that a competitor is willing to exert: with respect to a given economic opportunity, the more wealth a competitor has in hand at a given moment, the less Drive–Effort the opportunity will evoke. The particular function used for illustration is exponential, in accordance with the standard assumption about the incremental function of (Benthamite) diminishing marginal utility. But any monotonic downward-sloped function – equivalent to an increasing 'cost' of additional inputs of effort with increasing quantities of that input – would produce similar results.

The first comparison is between a given market when serviced by one versus two firms. A downward-sloping incremental Drive–Effort function with respect to additional net revenue, and a concave-downward total-revenue sales-response function with respect to successive amounts of effort expended (together with the plausible assumption that competitors obtain sales in proportion to the amounts of effort they expend) combine to imply that two competing firms will expend more effort than will one firm, even if the overall sales-response function passes through the origin. (This is unlike the case with advertising, which can be thought of as similar to the Drive–Effort analysis except that the 'cost' of incremental input is constant rather than increasing as is the case with effort; if the total-revenue function with respect to advertising passes through the origin, two competitors may be expected to advertise in total only as much as would a monopolist in this simple case.)

The reasons for the greater expenditure of effort in the divided-market case are:

> (1) The division of the market pushes competitors back to ranges of operation where they are poorer and therefore have a higher propensity to exert effort in order to obtain a given amount of net revenue. This conclusion follows from the combination of the Drive–Effort function and the total revenue function; neither alone is sufficient. If the *TR* function cuts the

vertical axis above the origin, then the conclusion follows *a fortiori*, and then the concave *TR* function is enough to lead to the conclusion, as is the case also with advertising.

(2) True competition rather than perfect co-operation gives each firm an incentive to expend effort in excess of the amount that would be expended in a co-operative solution. This follows from the definition of co-operation as firms acting in concert in such fashion as will maximize the welfare of the two taken together. The absence of such co-operation implies that one firm will assume that the competitor will *not* act in concert, and therefore the firm treats the competitor's position as at least temporarily fixed. If so, a move by one firm even from the joint-maximization point will be (at least temporarily) profitable for the other firm because the latter will receive returns as if it were a monopolist having the whole market; with this outlook, the marginal function at the joint-maximization point is steeper than if the outlook is for the firm with the competitor acting in concert. This is the mechanism of 'cheating' described and analysed convincingly by Stigler (1964).

In the case where the sales in a merged market are split by two competitors who each formerly monopolized the separated markets, if the two competitors co-operate perfectly there will be no increase in effort expended. But in the absence of perfect co-operation, each competitor has reason to expend effort beyond the co-operative amount, by exactly the same reasoning as in the divided-market case.

Concerning the outcomes if the firms have different Drive–Effort functions: I have no theory about the equilibrium the firms would reach even if they were to communicate with total honesty about future interactions and actions. Hence one cannot say whether the total effort under those circumstances would be greater, less, or the same as if the firms operated as monopolists in separated markets. But one can say that no matter what the equilibrium reached under such conditions, there would then be incentive for each of the competitors to expend greater effort if there were absence of perfect co-operation.

The reason for the great difference in results for the divided-market case versus the merged-market case is simply that in the former the monopolist is made poorer by the change, and this impoverishment leads rather straightforwardly to more effort. In the latter case, no such impoverishment takes place, and hence the outcome depends on various other conditions.

The chapter does not deal with the situation in which there may be a continuing attachment of customers to a seller from period to period, and the effect this may have upon a new entrant. This factor would be a considerable complication; it is difficult to analyse even where effort is not considered to be a variable. Eventually, however, it could be included in the analysis.

A major aim of this chapter is to demonstrate the usefulness of the Drive–Effort concept. The same concept seems to be useful for analysing issues as diverse as the rise and fall of empires, and the relationship of the number of children in a family to the amount of work done in the labour force by the father and the mother at various children's ages, as for the analysis of monopoly versus duopoly in this chapter.

Appendix: Notes on the Construction of the Incremental Drive–Effort Function

(1) The results of the calculations obviously depend on the procedure. Consider a decision-maker with $W_0 = \$100$, and $a = 2000$, deciding whether to expend 1500 units of effort which will produce $100. The calculation is

$$\text{IncDrEf} = 2000 \frac{(\$200 - \$100)}{\$100} = 2000,$$

and the opportunity will be accepted because $2000 > 1500$. If an additional 1500 units of effort will produce $50, the calculation for that decision will be

$$\text{IncDrEf} = 2000 \frac{(\$250 - \$200)}{\$200} = 500,$$

and the second unit of effort will not be expended because $500 < 1500$. (Notice, please, that the second calculation had $W_n = \$200$, including the $100 at the start of the decision-making plus the $100 obtained from the first unit of effort.

But now consider the calculation if the decision had been 3000 units of effort or none to obtain $150.

$$\text{IncDrEf} = 2000 \, \frac{(\$250 - \$100)}{\$100} = 3000,$$

and since IncDrEf is just equal to the necessary effort, the decision to expend both units of effort would be on the knife-edge.

(2) For a situation in which any amount of effort can be chosen, it is appropriate to use a continuous function, constructed operationally by considering successive very small increments of effort; this is the nature of the IncDrEf function in figure 6.1. (One might just as well do the calculations in fairly large increments, for convenience and because this is the way decision-makers act in most situations, in the same way that they decide, for example, whether to spend $500,000, or $750,000, or $1,000,000 for advertising, and not whether to spend $500,000, or $500,001, or $500,002 . . .)

(3) It does not make sense to draw a cumulative function for DrEf the way one constructs a function for the relationship between actual effort and sales. This is because there is no basis for adding the incremental DrEf that one is willing to expend to go from, say, $100 to $180 sales revenue, to the DrEf that one would have been willing to expend to get from $0 to $100 sales. The sum of those quantities is *not* the same as the amount of DrEf that one would be willing to expend to get from $0 to $180. There is no sensible way that one can construct a cumulative function from which one could determine the DrEf to get from any one revenue point to another.

Notes

1 This was shown by Stigler (1964), pp. 44–61; and Simon, Puig, and Aschoff (1973), pp. 353–66.

2 Alfred Marshall's comment about the classical writers is relevant in this connection: 'For the sake of simplicity of argument, Ricardo and his followers often spoke as though they regarded man as a constant quantity . . . It caused them to speak of labour as a commodity without staying to throw themselves into the point of view of the workman; and without dwelling upon the allowances to be made for his human passions, his instincts and habits, his sympathies and antipathies, his class jealousies and class adhesiveness, his want of knowledge and of the opportunities for free and vigorous action. They therefore attributed to the forces of supply and demand a much more mechanical and regular action than is to be found in real life.' (1920, pp. 762–3)

3   For example, see Baumol (1982); and Smith, Williams, Bratton, and Vannona (1982).
4   See Stigler (1964); Simon (1970), chapter 4; and especially Simon (1982).
5   For summaries of evidence about the shape of the analogous advertising-response function, see Simon (1965), and Simon and Arndt (1980). Contrary to common belief, the function is not S-shaped but rather is simply concave downward, as shown conclusively by a wide array of data of many kinds.
6   This latter case was incorrectly analysed in Simon (1967), pp. 610–62; and in Simon (1970), chapter 4.
7   As shown in Simon (1967), pp. 610–62; and in Simon (1970), chapter 4.
8   For discussion of this, see Stigler (1964); and Simon (1982).
9   A more rigorous and elegant proof for this section was developed by Salim Rashid, and is contained in an unpublished paper by Simon and Rashid with the same title as this chapter.

7

Applications to Macroeconomics and Economic Development

The applications of the Drive–Effort hypothesis discussed in chapters 7 and 8 are intended to show how the analysis helps us understand a wide range of phenomena. The applications discussed in the latter section of chapter 5 should also be considered as among the applications of the analysis. And of course the analysis of monopoly/duopoly in chapter 6 is a key application, worked out at length for demonstration purposes.

The applications fall into two general classes: (a) Applications which relate economic behaviour to wealth. In such cases, there is reasonable hope of being able to investigate the relationship quantitatively. (b) Applications which relate economic behaviour to changes in opportunities such as alterations in the tax or social structure, where establishing a quantitative relationship is more difficult and less likely, and we therefore probably must be content with qualitative discussion; yet this latter set of applications includes such large matters as the rise and fall of nations, which would seem of sufficient import for us to be willing to tolerate discussion that is looser than one would otherwise hope for.

The Rise and Fall of Empires

Explaining the decline of even a single empire – a better term is 'dominant nation', which would clearly include the United States after the Second World War even if the term 'empire' seems inappropriate – has been, and continues to be, one of the great intellectual tasks of all time, for example, Rome and Gibbon. A variety of explanations have been offered for each case. It would therefore be presumptuous in the extreme for anyone to claim, on the basis of a superficial examination of the historical facts, that a single line of explanation is a satisfactory explanation of even one case, let alone all the cases of declines of empires.

Yet if broad enough, a single organizing framework may be useful. From unsystematic reading I extract this broad outline: The fortunes of a given empire seen to be heavily influenced by (a) some combination of (i) the economic performance and output of the large proportion of its citizens (its 'average' income), together with (ii) the overall population size of the empire; and (b) the combination of the same factors of its antagonists. This assertion does not imply unimportance of ideological motivation, but it does suggest that ideology and culture are likely to be less continuingly dominant than are relative demography and economics.

If this broad framework is not totally unacceptable – and it is so broad that it seems to encompass the ideas of most writers on the subject – then it can be agreed that the economic fortunes of the dominant nation matter greatly. With this perspective, it is interesting to consult Cipolla's collection of essays on *The Economic Decline of Empires*. It would be naively imprudent to suppose that the selection of these essays might not have been affected by Cipolla's own point of view, as set forth cogently in his introduction. Yet it would be equally imprudent to assume that those essays, written by a variety of scholars considered well informed by their peers, should be dismissed as a source of information for testing one's theories and drawing own conclusions about the subject.

My reading of those essays, and of other accounts of imperial declines, supports the view that the combination of decreased economic opportunity and increased consumption for the large body of citizens is important. To exemplify with Rome: (a) following on increases in the standard of living from increased production; (b) transfers in money and kind to the lower-income citizens derived from the provinces grew so great that many citizens did not need to work in order to consume at a high level (bread and circuses), which implies a high level of effective 'wealth'; while (c) at the same time taxation on output grew, so that the opportunities for income and increased wealth were shrinking. (The increasing concentration of land ownership enters here, also.) This combination of increased average personal wealth of the lower-income class (from transfers) and decreased opportunity (due to taxes) implies less Drive–Effort, according to the framework set forth here. Less Drive–Effort on the part of the average citizen caused economic decline which, combined with a falling ratio of Roman citizens to the populations of contending nations, led to a shift in relative military as well as economic power. Military power was affected not only by the number of soldiers that could be mustered, but also by a reduction in Rome's capacity to pay them.

Venice in its heyday suffered problems because its populace was too prosperous to take some dirty jobs. Lane tells us that:

> A galley commander . . . about 1550 evaluated the kinds of free men available. Although he spoke well of Venetians serving as officers or able-bodied seamen, or even as marines, he considered the oarsmen recruited at Venice the worst. In so prosperous a city, good men found other jobs, only penniless beggars enlisted as oarsmen. (1973, p. 368)

Similar observations about the decline of empires have surely been made throughout history. In 1705 Mandeville observed about Spain:

> A man would be laughed at by most people who should maintain that too much money could undo a nation, yet this has been the fate of Spain; to this the learned Don Diego Saavedra ascribes the ruin of his country. The fruits of the earth in former ages had made Spain so rich that King Lewis XI of France being come to the court of Toledo was astonished at its Splendour and said that he had never seen anything to be compared to it, either Europe or Asia; he that in his travels to the Holy Land had run through every province of them. In the kingdom of Castile alone (if we may believe some writers), there were for the holy war from all parts of the world got together one hundred thousand foot, ten thousand horse, and sixty thousand carriages for baggage, which Alfonso III maintained at his own charge and paid every day, as well soldiers as officers and princes, every one according to his rank and dignity; nay down to the reign of Ferdinand and Isabella (who equipped Columbus) and some

time after, Spain was a fertile country, where trade and manufactures flourished, and had a knowing industrious people to boast of. But as soon as that mighty treasure that was obtained with more hazard and cruelty than the world until then had known and which to come at, by the Spaniards own confession, had cost the lives of twenty million of Indians; as soon, I say, as that ocean of treasure came rolling in upon them, it took away their senses, and their industry forsook them. The farmer left his plough, the mechanic his tools, the merchant his counting-house, and everybody scorning to work, took his pleasure and turned gentleman. They thought they had reason to value themselves above all their neighbours, and now nothing but the conquest of the world would serve them.

The consequences of this has been that other nations have supplied what their own sloth and pride denied them; and when everybody saw that notwithstanding all the prohibitions the government could make against the exportation of bullion, the Spaniard would part with his money and bring it [to] you aboard himself at the hazard of his neck, all the world endeavoured to work for Spain. Gold and silver being by this means yearly divided and shared among all the trading countries have made all things dear and most nations of Europe industrious, except their owners, who, ever since their mighty acquisitions, sit with their arms across and wait every year with impatience and anxiety the arrival of their revenues from abroad to pay others for what they have spent already; and thus by too much money, the making of colonies and other mismanagements, of which it was the occasion, Spain is from a fruitful and well-peopled country, with all its mighty titles and possessions, made a barren and empty thoroughfare through which gold and silver pass from America to the rest of the world; and the nation, from a rich, acute, diligent, and laborious, become a slow. idle, proud, and beggardly people. So much for Spain. (1705/1962, pp.123–5)

Modern historians apparently agree on these elements being present and influential during the period of Spanish decline: (a) increase in taxation, (b) lack of enterprise and hard work within large segments of the population, and (c) depopulation. The first of these elements constitutes a depressing effect upon effort because it depresses the value of opportunities. The second element is direct evidence of reduction in the key economic input at the individual level. And the third, depopulation, would seem to be both a sign of lack of effort (though this requires additional discussion, which is not likely to be conclusive) as well as indicating a reduction in gross output, which is perhaps the best measure of a country's strength when military action is part of the story of the nation's decline.

Increased and oppressive taxation appears prominently in the accounts of various nations' declines collected by Cipolla. As he summarizes:

> One of the remarkably common features of empires at the later stage of their development is the growing amount of wealth pumped by the State from the economy. In the later Roman Empire taxation reached such heights that land was abandoned and many peasants, after paying their rents or taxes, had too little food left to nourish their children. (1970, p .6)

And among all economic forces, taxation has the unusual characteristic in this context – especially in the Roman case – of having pernicious effects on both elements in the Drive–Effort concept. From one side, any taxation of production reduces economic opportunity by reducing the pay-off to particular actions, and thereby reduces Drive–Effort. From the other side, taxation that results in welfare transfers increases the wealth of many and thereby reduces their Drive–Effort. So such taxation has a scissors-like depressing effect upon economic activity in farming and elsewhere. (Different sorts of taxes can differ in their effects upon Drive–Effort, of course. This is discussed in the appendix to this chapter.)

Cipolla uses the term 'sclerotic' for the condition of the declining empires' economies, and Olson (1982) uses the same term in his analysis. A hallmark of such sclerosis certainly is insufficient change in ways of doing things. As Cipolla comments:

> At least in the early phase of a decline, however, the problem does not seem to be so much that of increasing visible inputs – capital or labour – as that of changing ways of doing things and improving productivity. The survival of the empire demands such basic change. But it is typical of mature empires to give a negative response to this challenge. (p. 7)

The analysis set forth here views any change as requiring effort. And interestingly, Cipolla uses the same word: 'Change implies imaginative effort' (p. 11). And he continues in a manner reminiscent of the Veblen quotations given earlier: 'Change hurts vested interests. It is not difficult to explain why change is generally opposed. It would be surprising if it were not. The tendency to resist change is strengthened by existing institutions.' The economic conditions leading to reduced Drive–Effort thereby lead to reduced change, which again fits the diagnosis of the causes of the decline of empires found in Cipolla's introduction and collected essays.

All in all, then, the Drive–Effort analysis seems to provide a useful organizing principle for the understanding of the decline of empires.

It probably is not accidental that the two developed countries whose recent economic rise was most rapid – West Germany and Japan – are also the two in which recent changes in Drive–Effort seem so marked. While after the Second World War those countries had to rebuild their physical plants for production and homes, and also had to re-establish themselves in foreign markets, their people exerted a great deal of effort in their work. With their success and affluence since then has come diminution in willingness to expend as much effort. The quotation on page 25 makes the point anecdotally for Japan. And an August 1984 news story says 'Japan Considering Plan to Shorten Workweek ... The proposal calls for cutting the workweek to 45 hours over five days from the current 48 hours over six days'.[1] With respect to West Germany, two surveys document a change between generations in the attitudes of Germans toward work. One study, done by Opaschowski and the Ernest Dichter Institut, found as follows:

> This study showed that about half the men in West Germany no longer find satisfaction in their jobs. They compensate by turning to leisure activities and elevating them to the central purpose in their life.   (E. Simon, 1982)

And the other study, done by Marplan Institut:

> Work dropped back from the traditional No. 1 spot to No. 4 on a scale asking the people interviewed to rate their most important desires and endeavors. The categories 'family and partnership', 'leisure time' and 'friends' ranked before 'work and career'. Of

those questioned, 85% put family and partnership in the No. 1 spot of 'most important concerns', 74% rated leisure in second place, friends in third and career in fourth place.

In previous generations, Germans admired career-mindedness and applauded success and dedication. Today, a person who knows how to use his leisure time to best advantage is assured admiration and popularity, Prof. Opaschowski says.

'The ideal German has changed', he adds. Only 20 years ago, people ranked industriousness and dedication to their job, ambition and achievement as desirable traits and the education of their children was patterned accordingly. The youngsters were given tasks early and learned that idleness was frowned on, even considered sinful.

Today's German parents want their children to have fun, to be cheerful and relaxed rather than concentrate on achievement.

(E. Simon, 1982).

The anecdote which characterized the report was this:

'Work? Sure I'll have to work, but work definitely will not be the most important aspect of my life', an 18-year-old carpenter's apprentice here told the interviewer emphatically.

'I don't want to be like my father. For him, work always came first and everything else ranged somewhere behind.

'As far as I am concerned, enjoying life will be the most important thing for me', he added.

Or consider this remark by Albert Shanker:

My kids don't work as hard in school as I worked. I got it from my mother and father every day: you are going to be a great student because otherwise you're going to be working like your father, seven days a week. I didn't do that with my children in my nice middle-class surburban neighborhood. The same pressure wasn't on them.

(*Washington Jewish Week*, 1 May 1986, p. 7)

The work week has shortened markedly in West Germany in recent years, from average actual hours per week of 38.8 in 1960–4 to 32.1 hours in 1982, as shown in Table 5.3. All components of work time have contributed – a decline in the standard work week, a decline in overtime, and an increase in time off for sickness and strikes. The work week is now comparable to that of other developed countries which did not suffer the war damage that West Germany suffered.

The economic histories of England and Germany in the second half of the nineteenth-century seem to fit neatly with this hypothesis, too. The United Kingdom had built itself a wealth of industrial plants, and therefore was less disposed to exert itself to build new factories than was Germany. And it is in the nature of things that later investment tends to be more efficient. So the result was not merely catch-up by Germany, but a surpassing of the United Kingdom.

Recent Income and Productivity Trends in the United States

We have heard a good deal in recent years to the effect that productivity and income have not risen as fast in the United States as in the other richest nations – that the United States now is behind Switzerland, Germany, etc. (which I doubt, however), and that absolute incomes in the United States have fallen. A deterioration in real income must spell a reduction in lifetime income (and therefore wealth) compared to earlier expectations. By the Drive–Effort hypothesis, this would suggest more effort than would otherwise have been expected. And indeed, there has been a 'back to basics'[2] movement in education and elsewhere. This movement includes a call for more discipline and harder work in schools and on the job.

History surely contains opposite cases wherein a decline in a country's performance was followed by a decline in effort. And there certainly are some forces, such as discouragement or consequent resignation, going in the opposite direction from the Drive–Effort hypothesis. It seems to me, however, that the Drive–Effort hypothesis might at least be used as just that – a hypothesis – one element (and perhaps the first element to be considered) in the analysis of such situations. If it turns out to aid our understanding of the observed facts, then we can rely on it more in the future; if not, it will soon drop out of the analytic kit used in such situations.

The issue of *relative* wealth arises when the trend in income in one country is compared to that in another country. There seems no more reason for a relativistic concept to affect the Drive–Effort Measure than there would be reason for the performance of another firm to affect a given firm's profit-maximizing calculation of the optimal price, say. Yet this seems insufficient, because relativistic comparisons do affect much human behaviour. This will have to be thought through more fully in the future. Perhaps seeing another country do better than on's own increases one's estimate of opportunities for achievement, just as achievement of the first four-minute mile showed many other runners that this was possible and thereby moved them to greater effort and greater achievement. In economics, this would translate into: 'They got rich, why can't I, too?' and such an increase in perceived opportunities may be an appropriate reinterpretation of what we often call a 'demonstration effect'. Of course, the excellent performances by others may increase performance of the person in question simply by making the person more 'competitive', as this term is usually used in sport.

The Effect of the Spanish New World on the Old World

Even while the Spanish galleons were hauling huge troves of silver and gold from the Americas to Seville, some students of the Spanish society and economy asked whether the treasure was having, on balance, a good or a bad effect upon Spain. As early as 1603, Justus Lipsius wrote to a Spanish friend that 'the New World, conquered by you, has conquered you in its turn' (quoted by Elliott, 1970, p. 63). Expanding on this theme about 1612, Garcilaso de la Vega wrote that 'this flood of riches has done more harm than good, since wealth commonly produces vice rather than virtue, inclining its possessors to pride, ambition, gluttony and voluptuousness . . . the riches of the New World . . . have . . . rendered men effeminate in their power of understanding and in their bodies, dress, and customs . . .' (quoted by Elliott, 1970, p. 64). This thought is also found in the 1705 quotation from Mandeville in the previous section. And in 1768, the celebrated Abbé Raynal sponsored an essay contest on the subject of whether the discovery of the Americas was on balance harmful or useful (Elliott, 1970, p. 1).

The effect upon Spain herself has already been analysed from the straightforward point of view of a decline in effort resulting from an increase in wealth. Whether the subsequent decline in income resulting from the decline in effort was less or more than the direct increase in income that the treasure represented is a question beyond the scope of the analysis; the answer must depend upon the other opportunities open to Spaniards in various years during and after the treasure-taking period, as well as upon a host of dynamic effects.

The effect upon countries *other than* Spain who were then competing with her, and the effect upon the aggregate of Spain and those other countries, must also be considered. And indeed, the 'increase in opportunity' for Europe as a whole has been pointed out by various writers (discussed by Elliott, 1970, p. 57). Mandeville's thought on the matter is clear and sharp in the above quotation. And even though the silver and gold brought back in by the Spaniards did not by itself affect the standard of living (except perhaps some of it used in ornamentation), the increase in total effort and consequent increase in economic activity generally could well have had a beneficial effect (together with psychological and organizational changes toward modernity that writers have suggested were important offshoots of the entire phenomenon; see Elliott, 1970, p. 57).

This effect can be illuminated by the Effort-Drive mechanism. The analysis assumes that the increase in wealth to Spain represents increased opportunity for the competing countries, constituting a stock of assets that the other countries could aspire to obtain through trade. (They could also aspire to obtain it by taking it in war, but that possibility may be left out of the discussion without hampering it.) This increased opportunity would induce increased effort on the part of those other countries, which tends to offset the decreased effort by the Spanish. The question then arises whether the *net* effect is increased or decreased effort.

Let us first assume that there is just one other relevant country along with Spain – call it NorthEur – and that it has the same wealth level, the same wealth distribution, and the same population size as Spain had before Spain acquired the treasure. Let us denote the increase in wealth from the American treasure by Z, the existing set of international opportunities facing both Spain and NorthEur by Y, and the wealth before the opening of the Americas by W. Then the results of Spain's treasure upon effort in the two countries may be calculated as follows:

We begin with the basic formulation

$$\text{DrEf} = \frac{W_1 - W_0}{W_0} \qquad (7.1)$$

Without considering the effects of treasure, $W_1 = W_0 + Y$.

We wish to contrast how the situation would be with the treasure as part of the picture against the situation with the treasure not part of the picture, and to calculate the difference between them by subtracting the latter from the former. For Spain,

$$\frac{(W_0 + Y + Z) - (W_0 + Z)}{W_0 + Z} - \frac{(W_0 + Y) - W_0}{W_0} \qquad (7.1a)$$

$$= \frac{-ZY}{W_0(W_0 + Z)}, \text{ the reduction in DrEf due to the treasure.}$$

For NorthEur,

$$\frac{(W_0 + Y + Z) - (W_0)}{(W_0)} - \frac{(W_0 + Y) - W_0}{W_0} \qquad (7.1b)$$

$$= \frac{Z(W_0 + Z)}{W_0(W_0 + Z)}, \text{ the increase in DrEf due to the treasure.}$$

Looking at the difference in the numerators — Y versus $(W_0 + Z)$ — we see that unless the set of other opportunities Y facing the countries is greater than $(W_0 + Z)$, the sum of the original wealth plus the treasure, the gain in effort propensity by NorthEur exceeds the loss in effort propensity by Spain.

But this is not the end of the story. If there are, say, two countries rather than one country like NorthEur, then the same amount of treasure obtained by Spain will serve as a stimulus to both of them, and there will be (say) twice as much additional effort induced outside Spain. And so on with more competing countries. So in the realistic case of the treasure being eyed by populations many times the size of Spain's, it is all the more plausible that the effort induced in them will outweigh the decline in effort in Spain.

The analysis given here is meant only to be suggestive, showing how there is at least the possibility of an effort trade-off inside and outside Spain, and illustrating how the Drive–Effort analysis can at least clarify such far-ranging problems that are difficult to think about systematically.

Effort, Economic Development, and Property Rights

A country's economic development obviously must be influenced greatly by the extent of the effort exerted by its citizens. And those who desire a country's economic development are necessarily concerned with policies that will elicit more rather than less effort. If we assume that the distribution of individuals' wealth is fixed at a given moment and therefore wealth is not a policy variable (which it might be in some schemes of income redistribution not to be considered here), then one's mind turns to the opportunity aspect of the Drive–Effort formulation. And indeed, for untold generations many writers have asserted that the best policy is to 'privatize' the means of production in order to 'internalize' the returns to effort to the largest possible degree. But this proposition does not have universal acclaim within the present conceptual framework, and it is worth asking why this proposition has not been acclaimed by all.

The difference on this matter between the classical school of Mandeville and Hume and Smith on the one side, with Godwin and Marx and modern socialists on the other side, hinges on whom the concept of opportunity refers to. Ordinarily there is no confusion about this; we assume it refers to the individual who will do the work and get paid, or perhaps to that individual plus her/his family. But for Marx et al., the reference implicitly is to a class or to an entire nation. And implicitly they assume that motivation is not less if the pay-off will be distributed among the wider group rather than kept by the worker and his family. (Socialist *practice* is different, however. More recently, 'As of August 1965, some 63 per cent of production workers in the Soviet Union were paid by some form of piecework with almost one-quarter working by straight piecework methods. In the 1950s, up to 42 per cent of China's industrial force were on piecework' (Pencavel, 1977, p. 231). And China has recently moved back toward piecework again, after the use of piecework methods declined in the 1960s.)

Hume and Smith and their colleagues were at bottom interested in human nature, and it was their interest in human nature that originally led them to the study of economics. They believed that human nature was roughly constant from time to time and place to place, and they assumed that the motivations that they observed –

personal economic interest among them – would remain much the same except in exceptional conditions. In contrast, Godwin and Marx and their followers believed that human nature is relatively malleable. And for them, the maximand may be the welfare of the class or nation rather than of the individual, in which case the concept of opportunity in the Drive–Effort Measure refers to that group's opportunity rather than to the opportunity of the individual.

It would seem that by 1986 enough evidence has accumulated to prove that the view of Hume and Smith is sound; group motivations are ineffective except temporarily during times of national emergency. This conclusion may be read in the comparative data on the economic development of socialist and enterprise economies, and agricultural production in the two sorts of countries, as well as in accounts of collective agriculture in China by Butterfield (1982), Mosher (1983), and others. The current leaders of the People's Republic of China apparently agree, given their post-1978 economic policy decisions.

From this follows the inference that the most effective mode of organization for economic development is to make the individual's pay-off situation coincide with an individual concept of opportunity, that is, to fix property rights with the individual to the maximum extent possible. This is, of course, exactly the programme of writers on development such as Bauer (e.g. 1984). But privatizing does not resolve the problem for socialist countries; private production property seems to be inconsistent in the long run with central planning and with the socialist form of political organization, because private property leads to centres of power emerging which challenge economic and political centralization (and if this is true, the recently announced Chinese reforms will be shortlived).

Johnson (1982) finds that in agriculture it is not the actual ownership of land that matters, at least in principle; the state is not necessarily a less effective landlord for a farmer than is a private owner. What does matter is that the agriculturalist has property rights over his or her produce. (Johnson says that the typical low productivity of agriculture in socialist economies is a result of the conditions in the socialist economies as wholes, and agriculture's relationship to markets for inputs and outputs and to non-agricultural sectors.) In China, 'grain production per capita in 1977 was the same as in 1957, and . . . as in 1936' (p. 849).

Climate and Economic Development

Why did modern economic development begin and continue primarily in moderate climes rather than in tropic or arctic regions? A common explanation has been that, unlike the tropics, the moderate climes provided 'enough' challenge to survival, but that unlike arctic regions, the challenge to mere survival was not so great as to make impossible efforts beyond those intended for the simplest survival. This idea (at least the first part of it) was stated nicely by the incomparable Hume:

> What is the reason why no people living between the tropics could ever yet attain to any part of civility or reach even any police in their government and any military discipline, while few nations in the temperate climates have been altogether deprived of these advantages? It is probable that one cause of this phenomenon is the warmth and equality of weather in the torrid zone, which render clothes and houses less requisite for the inhabitants and thereby remove, in part, that necessity which is the great spur to industry and invention. *Curis acuens mortalia corda.* Not to mention that the fewer goods or possessions of this kind any people enjoy, the fewer quarrels are likely to arise amongst them, and the less necessity will there be for a settled police or regular authority to protect and defend them from foreign enemies or from each other. (1953, p. 141)

This line of thinking can be made more systematic with the Drive–Effort analysis. Before economic development begins, effective wealth is greater in the tropics than in moderate climes, because easy sources of food and of sufficient shelter against the elements constitute a natural endowment of wealth, in the best sense of that term. But there is considerable opportunity to increase 'income' and the standard of living in the moderate climes, and not necessarily a great deal less such opportunity than in the tropic climes. Hence the Drive–Effort Measure may be seen as greater in moderate climes than in the tropics.

In the arctic regions, there is little opportunity for economically-primitive people to improve their standard of living significantly, because of the arctic regions' paucity of natural resources that can be developed without high technology. Though wealth endowment there also is low, there would seem to be a smaller gap between opportunity and wealth in the arctic than in moderate climes, and hence more drive for development in the moderate climes than in arctic regions.

Of course these statements – made without recourse to conceptual measurements of opportunity and wealth, let alone actual measurements – can be only impressions, and another observer could argue for opposite impressions and conclusions. Yet the Drive–Effort analytic scheme may at least be of value in focusing this argument on measurements that may help one reach more defensible conclusions on this perennial question.

Natural Resource Exploitation and Economic Development

A great economic paradox: humans seem to be using up natural endowments of such resources as copper, coal and oil, which would threaten to choke off further economic advance, yet economic advance continues, and resources have shown a long secular trend towards more availability rather than less, as measured by the costs and prices of these resources (Barnett and Morse, 1963; Simon, 1981).

Part of the explanation lies in the fact that when a resource becomes more scarce for a while, as indicated by rising prices, there occurs in that industry and in related industries both an increased opportunity (due to the higher price) and decreased wealth (due to the higher costs of inputs, and therefore probably a lower profit). The increased Drive–Effort Measure induces greater efforts to find substitutes than existed heretofore, and therefore the increased scarcity usually results in substitutes being found.[3]

Why the *long run* result of the expected or felt scarcity is that the resource in question – now suitably broadened in definition to include its substitutes, as when coal and then oil substituted for wood as fuel, and fuel replaced wood as a concept with respect to heating – eventually comes to be lower in price than before the price run-up, is a story beyond this chapter, and a speculative one at that. Key elements are that (a) one scarcity-forced discovery leads to other discoveries which are not forced by scarcity in the same way, and which therefore are a bonus; and (b) raw material substitution is simpler than substitution of one consumer good for another because of the simpler taste-free nature of natural resources.

Absence of natural resources also reduces a group's wealth endowment, which therefore should increase its level of effort. Bishop George Berkeley in 1735 wondered 'Whether a discovery of the richest gold mine that ever was, in the heart of the kingdom, would be a real advantage to us? . . . Whether it would not render us a lazy, proud, and dastardly people?' (Quoted by Stigler and Friedland on a calendar) Perhaps he had in mind the experience of Spain, as discussed by Mandeville a few years earlier (see page 115). Nowadays the Japanese see themselves in this way, with land shortage being the lack of a natural resource that they say has driven them to their economic success. And certainly the recent experiences of Hong Kong and Singapore square with this view.

Economic Development and Availability of Goods

Consider this apparent contradiction in the theory of historical and contemporary economic development: Making goods available for purchase by consumers is commonly thought to stimulate additional effort, to satisfy the desire to purchase these goods; this is often known as the 'Sears Roebuck Wishbook effect'. This proposition was clearly stated as far back as Hume, who wrote:

> When a nation abounds in manufactures and mechanic arts, the proprietors of land, as well as the farmers, study agriculture as a science and redouble their industry and attention. The superfluity which arises from their labor is not lost, but is exchanged with manufactures for those commodities which men's luxury now makes them covet. (1953, p. 135)

And Dudley North, (in *Discourses Upon Trade*, 1691) referred to 'the exhorbitant Appetites of Man' as the main spur to 'Industry and Ingenuity'; saying 'Did Men content themselves with bare necessaries, we should have a poor World.' (Quoted by Briggs, 1983, p. 162)

On the other hand, a lower effective price of consumer goods increases effective wealth. The Drive–Effort analysis clarifies the matter, even though it does not immediately predict the outcome of the process. The result of these opposing forces is a trade-off, analogous to the trade-off that may result in a backward-bending labour supply curve (discussed at more length on page 000): on the one hand, an increased wage increases the value of the opportunity to work a given incremental hour; on the other hand, after a given number of hours the worker is wealthier than with a lower wage. The trade-off between the two effects with respect to a particular quantity of work is not determined without additional information. There must, however, be *some* point at which the supply curve bends backward, because wealth increases with the quantity of hours worked whereas opportunity does not.

Social and Economic Stability–Instability

McNeill (1963), Jones (1981) and others have suggested that over several centuries the relative instability of social and economic life in Europe, compared with China and India, helps account for the emergence of modern growth in the West rather than in the East.[4] This idea may be understood in terms of the Drive–Effort hypothesis: instability implies economic disequilibria, which (as Schultz reminds us, 1975) imply exploitable opportunities which then lead to augmented effort. (Such disequilibria also cause the production of new knowledge, if the hypothesis offered here is correct.)

The conclusion of this analysis is nicely consistent with the thrust of Braudel's work, as summarized in a recent review by Hoelterhoff:

'The important thing', he writes, 'was the long period of pressure after the 13th century which raised the level of its material life and transformed its psychology.' A combination of energy, need and possibility of profit pushed Europe beyond its doors. (1982, p. 24)

Nicely said: need and possibility. That is, reduced wealth per family (especially land holdings) because of population growth, together with increased opportunities due to the secular economic boom plus urbanization, caused an increase in Drive–Effort.

People frequently inquire why, if more people cause there to be more ideas and knowledge, and hence higher productivity and income, India and China are not the richest nations in the world. Let us put aside the point that size in terms of population within national boundaries was not very meaningful in earlier centuries when national integration was much looser than it is now. There remains the question, however, why so many human beings in those countries produced so little change in the last few hundred years. In earlier writing I suggested that low education of most people in China and India prevented them from producing knowledge and change, though noting the very large (in absolute terms) contemporary scientific establishments in those two countries. But though education may account for much of the present situation, it does not account nearly as well for the differences between the West and the East over the five centuries or so up to, say, 1850.

The hypothesis that the combination of a person's wealth and opportunities affect the person's exertion of effort may go far in providing an explanation. *Ceteris paribus*, the less wealth a person has, the greater the person's drive to take advantage of economic opportunities. The village millions in India and China certainly have had plenty of poverty to stimulate them. But they lacked opportunities because of the static and immobile nature of their village life. In contrast, villagers in Western Europe apparently had more mobility, less stability, and more exposure to cross-currents of all kinds.

Just why Europe should have been so much more open is a question that historians answer with conjectures about religion, smallness of countries with consequent competition and instability, and a variety of other special conditions. The key matter for our purposes here, however, is not the causes of the differences in stability and openness, but rather the fact that the differences existed. If so, the differences imply relative lack of opportunities in the East, and hence help explain the relative stagnation there.

A corollary, of course, is that once the people in the East lose the shackles of static village life, and get some education, their poverty (absolute and relative) will drive them to an extraordinary explosion of creative effort. The happenings in Taiwan and Korea in recent decades suggest that this is already beginning to occur.

This explanation would seem more systematic, and more consistent with the large body of economic thought, than are explanations in terms of Confucianism or particular cultures, just as the Protestant-ethic explanation for the rise of the West (discussion of which goes back at least to Hume) now seems unpersuasive in the face of religious counter-examples (for example, the Catholic Ibo in Nigeria) and shifts in behaviour of Protestant nations.

Necessity as the Mother of Invention

How can one explain the development, only after adversity's onset, of technology which would have been profitable before the onset of adversity? For example, better scheduling methods for airline flights were developed very soon after the United States air controllers struck work in 1981, though the methods could have been discovered and used earlier. Relevant here is Samuel Johnson's famous saying that 'when a man knows he is to be hanged in a fortnight, it concentrates his mind wonderfully'. Adverse conditions may be interpreted as a state of lower wealth, in the generalized sense of lessened command over economic goods, which then leads to increased effort in creating and adopting new ideas.

Robinson Crusoe is the classic story of how sudden impoverishment leads to a burst of creativity. (Economists commonly refer to Crusoe to illustrate allocation of resources, but the allocation process is not the central element in the Crusoe story; rather, invention is at its heart.)

A typical historical example of the relationship between necessity and discovery is the story of Marco Polo's father and uncle creating a new trade route for Venice. As Lane (1973, p. 80) tells the story:

> Nicolo and Matteo Polo . . . were among the Venetians who, after setting up business in Constantinople, extended their commerce across the Black Sea to Soldaia on the southern tip of the Crimea. In 1260 they decided to explore commercial possibilities further inland. Taking jewels and some other wares they rode from Soldaia to Sarai (near modern Saratow) on the Volga River, the capital of the Golden Horde. It proved to be a very good time indeed to be away from Constantinople and out of the Black Sea, since it was precisely in July, 1261, that the Greeks retook Constantinople and encouraged the eager Genoese to seize all the Venetians they could. Some fifty Venetians were captured trying to escape from the Black Sea

and treated by the Greek emperor as pirates, being punished by blinding and having their nose cut off. How much the Polo brothers heard of this, possibly exaggerated, can only be imagined, but it seems an adequate reason why they should not try to go back by the way they had come, although it is not the reason given by Nicolo's son, Marco Polo, who wrote of their travels. Even Sarai may have seemed unsafe if the Polo brothers were sufficiently informed, for the Greek empire became for a few years the connecting link in an alliance with the Golden Horde on the one side and the Mamluks on the other, an alliance directed partially against the Khanate of Persia and partially against Venice. It is ironic but typical of the commercial conditions of the period that the coup at Constantinople in 1261, a commercial disaster for the Venetians, should have set in motion the finding of a new route and the most celebrated of all Venetian journeys.

Another example is the behaviour of the Chinese toward new developments in chronology. The emperor turned down a gift of watches from King George III of England, together with a quid pro quo of trade with that country, saying: 'We have never set much store on strange and ingenious objects, nor do we need any more of your country's manufactures' (quoted by Landes, 1983, p. 49). China thought itself to be the centre of the world, having all the things that it needed. And as Landes put it, 'good enough is the enemy of good' (p. 29).

A more modern example of the same principle is the reaction of firms in countries that joined the Common Market and no longer were protected. Before the change, one observer noted, 'If you don't care about competition, you don't care about quality. There is no stimulus for innovating.'[5]

War, Necessity and Opportunity

In wartime, civilians exert more effort than in peacetime – more work hours on the job, higher labour-force participation, and probably a higher rate of innovation in order to cope with unusual wartime job and personal demands.

One may view the additional work effort in wartime as a response to patriotic sentiments and appeals. But the additional time spent in keeping body and soul together, and the coping effort expended in innovation, can also be interpreted as a response to the combination of reduced wealth (for example, rations smaller than in peacetime, and shortages of housing and other goods) and of greater opportunities (grey markets, for example) due to breakdown of the usual organization of society, and the absence of the persons who usually fill various market roles.

A greater flow of innovations on the job probably occurs in wartime due to greater receptivity to innovations and greater reward to the innovators (that is, greater opportunities) due to war. But the climate for innovations also must be more receptive because a nation's wealth is reduced in wartime, by the very nature of its competition for survival.

Nef argues that the overall advance of knowledge is not greater during wartime than in peacetime (1950/1963). But his argument concerns the *type* of knowledge produced during wartime more than the amount of it, so his argument need not be taken as rebuttal to what is being said here.[6]

Population Push and Subsistence Agriculture

Boserup (1965) and many anthropologists[7] have shown how subsistence agriculturalists shift to production methods that require more labour per unit of output when population grows and the old techniques do not produce 'enough' food per person due to reduction in land per family.[8] This shift in time allocation may be viewed as a response to reduced wealth in land per family, or as a response to a reduction in the income stream from the family's land using the old technique. This shift in time allocation fits the analysis offered here, though it could also be seen as simply an implication of Becker's analysis. However, the shift in technique also requires an adjustment effort apart from the additional work time involved, and only the analysis offered here implies that that would happen. Therefore, it would seem that the Drive–Effort analysis is a reasonable framework for understanding the shifts in subsistence-agricultural techniques taken as a whole.

Population Growth Through Natural Increase

In a straightforward arithmetic fashion, additional children in a family reduce assets per person. For example, either there is less housing space per person when the family is larger, or the family must expend wealth to acquire additional housing in order to maintain the pre-existing level. So faster population growth by way of higher fertility should increase Drive–Effort by way of the wealth effect.

An increase in the size of the working population (which does not happen for some years after children are born, but inevitably occurs eventually if births increase) also increases opportunities for producers in all industries (especially agriculture) due to larger demand and perhaps higher prices. There may be decreased opportunity for children in families that have $n + 1$ instead of n children due to reduced nutrition and education. In economically advanced countries the nutrition effect is not likely to be important. The extent to which the education effect operates is in some doubt but would not be difficult to measure.[9]

The Consequences of Immigration

The Drive–Effort hypothesis illuminates two aspects of migration, its causes and its consequences. This section considers the latter, and a section in chapter 8 considers the former, though limited to the country of destination.

Immigration has the same positive effects upon the 'average' Drive–Effort in a society as does population growth from natural increase. And immigration clearly lacks the alleged (but mostly non-existent) negative effect of additional births through reduced nutrition and education, because the immigrants are only present after, and not while, their nutrition and education might be affected.

Furthermore, because the country of immigration usually is richer than the country of origin, the migrant's tangible wealth is likely to be less than the average tangible wealth of the natives of the country of immigration, and immigrants are not entitled to the same welfare programmes, all of which should mean higher average Drive–Effort by immigrants than by natives. The consequent increase in a nation's average 'stock' of Drive–Effort by immigration therefore seems clear-cut. And this phenomenon seems evident in the jobs that immigrants do. For example, judging from such cities as Washington, New York, Chicago, and Melbourne, immigrants have a very high propensity to be taxi drivers. There would seem to be no other likely explanation than that immigrants are more willing to work hard, and more willing to work for earnings which depend on their output. And while my evidence is skimpy, it also appears that immigrants have a tendency to seek out jobs as domestics, which require a certain amount of enterprise. For example, of the first thirteen advertisees my family phoned in the Washington area, twelve were immigrants.

A vivid case of immigrant effort and its results occurred in the shrimping industry in Texas:

> 'The Vietnamese shrimper is one tough competitor. He's rugged. He don't listen to the weatherman or go by any work schedule. He's out there day and night, dragging the bay.'
>
> 'And the SOB, he can live on practically nothing.' ...
>
> The story of the Vietnamese takeover of shrimping here is in many ways the classic American immigrant saga. They came, they toiled, they sacrificed, they overcame hostility and violence, they prevailed.[10]

A large literature on immigrants' earnings over the years in the United States, beginning with Chiswick's work, systematically supports the idea that immigrants work harder than natives, though self-selection may be part of the explanation.

A variety of data (see summary in Simon, forthcoming, chapter 4) show: (a) a larger proportion of 'ethnics' than of natives operated small businesses in the United States early in this century, and (b) a relatively high proportion of Asian immigrants in Canada and Australia have operated their own firms in recent years.

The Division of Labour is Limited by the Diversity of the Market

Adam Smith's proposition about division of labour and the *extent* of the market assumed that a bigger market simply implied more of the *same* commodity – standardized pins, for example. It is an important shortcoming of Smith's discussion (as Menger pointed out long ago, 1871/1981), that Smith proposed division of labour as the main force causing economic development, without including technical change (and especially endogenous technical change) in the main line of his analysis.

In this section I emphasize still another element not found in Smith's analysis: a larger market implies a wider *variety* of customers to whom one may sell one's goods, with a wider variety of tastes than does a smaller market. This implies that in a larger rather than a smaller market, any given owner of unique skills (such as playing the balalaika, or organizing the books in a library) has a better chance of finding a customer for that skill, and a better chance of finding a customer who will value that skill highly. This immediately implies that sellers' incomes will be higher, on average, where there is a larger variety of sellers and buyers due to the increased opportunities. Furthermore, the wider set of opportunities will lead to new skills being developed.

To put the matter differently, the size of the market affects economic development in ways other than greater specialization leading to faster work. Where the market is larger, there will be more learning-by-doing because more skills are in use, as new skills are grafted onto the old skills. And new skills will be developed to serve more opportunities. The effect of an increase in Drive–Effort due to increased opportunities is in the same direction. So, assuming that a larger population does not result in lower average income as it leads to larger total income during the relevant period, larger population size implies faster economic development for the reasons given above, as well as by way of a larger supply of inventive minds and through the productivity-increasing effect of larger volume in various industries (the latter, of course, being closely related to other factors discussed above). All of this surely would come clearer with detailed formal analysis.

Following from the above considerations, the Drive–Effort hypothesis contains a further implication for the comparison of markets by size: the more attractive set of opportunities offered by the larger market will induce more effort from potentially productive persons.

Appendix: Drive–Effort and Varieties of Taxes

Different sorts of taxes can be seen to have different effects within the Drive–Effort framework; some affect wealth, while others affect opportunity. The effects go in opposite directions, as discussed in the standard literature on taxation.

A property tax such as a hearth tax, found in China and in England in earlier years, reduces wealth and therefore increases Drive–Effort; the same is true of a head tax such as was used in Africa by British colonial administrators for this very purpose of getting the 'natives' to work harder, rather than for the revenue itself.

An income tax, in contrast, has a depressing effect upon Drive–Effort, and upon expended effort and work time, because it reduces the pay-off to any particular opportunity. A recent study of the 1981 US tax cut estimated 'that perhaps one-quarter to one-third of the increased reporting of income was due to increased *effort*, while the remainder was due to other forms of taxpayer behaviour' (Lindsey, 1986, p. 26). A proportional tax upon a subsistence farmer's agricultural output is very much like an income tax in this respect. Of course a higher income tax also means that less wealth will be accumulated, but in the context of subsistence agriculture in Europe or elsewhere, this effect is not likely to be important, especially because a (the?) major wealth holding was (is) land, and the total amount of land owned does not vary enormously in a short period of time, even though it may change hands.

The value of land tends to be a constant multiple of gross output – about 3.5 to 1 – as Clark's historical-geographic survey (1957) suggests. If this ratio holds for gross output less an output tax, a reduction in such a 'residual' due to an increase in taxes would leave the Drive–Effort Measure unchanged, because both numbers in the numerator and the one number in the denominator are changed in the same proportion. And if the farmer were to hire labour rather than work the farm with only the family's labour, the value of the land should go down more than proportionately with an output tax, because net profit for the land would go down faster, and would reach zero profits at far less than 100 per cent taxation. This would imply an effort-inducing effect of an output tax on agriculture. But such a hired-inputs situation is not representative of subsistence agriculture.

Satisfactory theoretical analysis of the effect of a proportional output tax in subsistence agriculture would be difficult to develop. It would have to take into account non-linear (concave-downward) relationships of effort and time to output, the linear tax itself, the size of the farmer's wealth (including human capital) other than land ownership, and the marginal utility of various amounts of food (which is likely to be perceived as some sort of a production target, 'enough' to feed the family). Given the difficulty of this theoretical analysis, it behoves us to examine empirical evidence. Judging from reports on Spain in the days of its empire, as well as the Roman Empire, increases in output taxation led to abandonment of farms and rural depopulation. This suggests that the outcome is less work time and effort in this key sector of the economy than would be exerted otherwise.

One curious income tax implication of the DrEf hypothesis deserves a word in passing. In Hayek's words:

> . . . if we were to follow up the implications of the contention that the utility of income in terms of effort is decreasing, we would arrive at curious conclusions. It would, in effect, mean that, as a person's income grows, the incentive in terms of additional income which would be required to induce the same marginal effort would increase. This might lead us to argue for regressive taxation, but certainly not for progressive. (1960, p. 309)

That is, taking a dollar's worth of goods from a poor person and giving it to a rich person (or even destroying it) would increase the total supply of effort, *ceteris paribus*. But Hayek goes on:

> It is, however, scarcely worthwhile to follow this line of thought further. There can now be little doubt that the use of utility analysis in the theory of taxation was all a regrettable mistake (in which some of the most distinguished economists of the time shared) and that the sooner we can rid ourselves of the confusion it has caused, the better. (1960, p. 309)

The main reason for Hayek's rejection of this line of thinking is that he was focusing on the consumption aspect of taxation here, together with his belief that 'the possibility of comparing the utilities to different persons has been generally abandoned' (p. 309). This would not apply to the DrEf hypothesis, which deals with phenomena more measurable than 'utility' (on which see Simon, 1974). But regressive taxation is quite unappealing on other grounds, and need not be discussed further here.

Notes

1 *Wall Street Journal*, 30 August 1984, p. 22.
2 I take the term from the title of Pines's book (1982), which is rather persuasive in urging the existence of such a trend.
3 It should be noted, however, that those firms outside the resource

industry which have no prospects of profiting by finding a substitute for the material in question suffer both decreased wealth (due to higher input costs of the material in question) and poorer opportunities (because of the overall change to the economy, as was the case in the United States after the oil price rise beginning in 1973). Hence the aggregate effect of increased scarcity of the natural resource is likely to be economic retrogression in the short run.

4   In a more recent work (1980) McNeill also offers as partial explanations the lack of oppressive tax structure, and political fragmentation of Europe with consequent market orientation. These factors increase economic opportunities.

5   Fernando Maravali, quoted in *Wall Street Journal*, 14 October 1985, p. 1.

6   In my senior year in college in 1953, I argued about this issue in a series of meetings with William Verplanck, my first-semester senior thesis adviser. I have become more agnostic on the subject since then (as with many other matters).

7   See summary by Pingali and Binswanger (1984).

8   For a geometric and arithmetic exposition, and an analysis of the conditions under which Boserup's theory does and does not apply, see Simon (1977b).

9   In this connection, see Simon and Pilarski (1979).

10 'Vietnamese Shrimpers Alter Texas Gulf Towns', *Washington Post*, 26 December 1984, pp. A1, A6.

8

Applications to Microeconomics and Work Behaviour

Backward-Bending Labour-Supply Curve

The underlying idea was clearly stated by Mandeville:

> Everybody knows that there is a vast number of journeymen weavers, tailors, cloth-workers, and twenty other handicrafts, who, if by four days labor in a week they can maintain themselves, will hardly be persuaded to work the fifth; and that there are thousands of laboring men of all sorts, who will, though they can hardly subsist, put themselves to fifty inconveniences, disoblige their masters, pinch their bellies, and run in debt to make holidays. When men show such extraordinary proclivity to idleness and pleasure, what reason have we to think that they would ever work unless they were obliged to it by immediate necessity? When we see an artificer that cannot be drove to his work before Tuesday because Monday morning he has two shillings left of his last week's pay, why should we imagine he would go to it at all if he had fifteen or twenty pounds in his pocket? (1705/1962, p. 122)

The Drive–Effort hypothesis, as discussed in the section in chapter 7 on 'Economic Development and the Availability of Goods', seems to explain this phenomenon more clearly than does the standard literature.[1].

A Richer View of Work Time and Leisure Time

Becker classes time into two categories – work time, and time spent in consumption. Introduction of the notion of effort permits a more flexible classification, which helps explain additional phenomena.

Consider a policeperson offered a second job as a security guard. He or she may turn down the job on the grounds that being on one's feet an extra four hours is too much. The job-offerer then suggests that the policeperson may sit in an easy chair while on the second job, and thereby rest from the first job. The offer is accepted. Is the second job work or leisure? The matter is clarified when we perceive the offer with the easy chair as requiring less effort than without it. Similarly, a physician may regretfully decide not to take a vacation trip to China, but on seeing an advertisement by a travel company for a free China trip for a doctor, then decides to go. Is the trip work or leisure? The free trip may be seen as a better opportunity than the paid vacation, thereby inducing more DrEf.

Minimum Wage Increase

Some writers have speculated that a rise in the minimum wage can increase worker effort with a 'shock effect' (see Brown et al., 1982, pp. 489–90). Expressed casually, the idea is that this makes the worker's job more valuable. This can be seen in the DrEf framework as an increase in opportunity, both because the job is more valuable and because finding another job is made harder by the minimum wage rise.

Labour-Force Participation and Marital Status

Married men living with a wife have much higher unadjusted rates of labour-force participation than do never-married, divorced, separated, or widowed men. Bowen and Finegan (1969) found that not all the difference in participation, or the parallel difference in hours worked, is explained by being married with a spouse present, but at least *some* of the large difference may be so explained.

Bowen and Finegan (1969, pp. 48–9) use the concept of family 'responsibilities' and a consequent 'taste for work' as their theoretical explanation. But the hypothesis of greater Drive–Effort as a result of lower wealth per person in the family would seem more satisfactory than those concepts.

Labour-Force Participation of Various Classes of Persons

The Drive–Effort concept, using as an argument wealth *per person* in the family, also seems useful for understanding a wide variety of other labour-force participation behaviour analysed by Bowen and Finegan, including lower participation by men whose wives work, higher participation by men with children, higher participation by women with older children than without such children, and so on. For example:

(1) Labour-force participation of males over 65 fell sharply from 68.3 per cent in 1900 to a bit over 20 per cent in 1975 (1969, p. 561) (see also Samuelson, 1978). The large rise in recent years in assets held by older persons – including Social Security entitlements – provides a straightforward explanation in terms of the simplest Hicksian time theory as well as the Drive–Effort hypothesis. (But see Jansen, as referred to by Hamermesh, 1984.)

(2) The higher labour-force participation of non-white females than of white females (Bowen and Finegan, 1969, p. 546) rather clearly is due to lower wealth, as measured by expected total future income of the family, of the former compared to the latter.

(3) Fewer widowed, divorced, and separated women participate in the labour force than do never-married women (Bowen and Finegan, 1969, p. 544). How much of this is due to greater wealth of the former (from insurance, alimony, etc.), and how much to greater opportunities of the latter due to more education or work experience or other factors, is an interesting question that could be answered empirically; it is an example of many such questions raised by the Drive–Effort analysis that hopefully will stimulate empirical analysis.

The Causes of International Migration

Demographers have long talked about international migration in terms of the 'push' in the country of origin and the 'pull' from the country of destination. In the words of Marc Lescarbot, a Frenchman writing in 1609 about migration to the New World, 'Three things induce men to seek distant lands and to leave their native homes. The first is the desire for something better. The second is when a province is so inundated with people that it overflows... The third is divisions, quarrels and lawsuits' (quoted by Elliott, 1970, p. 76). The Americas offered extraordinary new possibilities of something better, and therefore induced many persons to make the extraordinary effort required to take ship and depart one's native lands for the fearsome unknown of an unsettled land. The population increase in Europe that was felt in the 1500s undoubtedly contributed an additional element of push.

In the Drive–Effort framework, the push of immigrants from the old country may be interpreted as the state of wealth, and the pull from the new country may be interpreted as opportunity. This conceptualization brings the phenomenon of international migration from the realm of *ad hoc* hypothesis into a more systematic framework of incentives.

Entrepreneurship and Effort

The Drive–Effort analysis helps explain the activity of entrepreneurs. First let us consider the characteristics of the entrepreneur as described by Schumpeter:

> [T]here is the will to conquer: the impulse to fight, to prove onself superior to others, to succeed for the sake, not of the fruits of success, but of success itself ... Finally, there is the joy of creating, of getting things done, or simply of exercising one's energy and ingenuity.　　　(Quoted by Hagen, 1975, p. 270)

Hagen's review of the various relevant literatures revealed findings 'entirely consistent with Schumpeter's characterization of motives' (p. 270). Hagen's generalization about the background of these entrepreneurial persons is that they come from groups 'who were not fully accepted socially by the leaders of their societies and who had reason to feel unjustly or unreasonably derogated' (p. 276).

Hagen emphasizes the psychological aspects. I would emphasize, rather, that social status must be closely related to economic security. Those who are derogated and despised are more likely to feel economically insecure than are other persons, having greater fear of arbitrary confiscation and discrimination than are other persons. (The experience of Indians in various African countries since independence illustrates this situation.) This economic view could help account for the parental teaching of outsider children about achievement motivation: 'You've got to be twice as good to get the same job.'

In brief, classes of persons producing relatively large numbers of entrepreneurs apparently have relatively low perceived wealth as measured by the subjective sense of economic security. By the Drive–Effort hypothesis, this implies additional effort, which is a hallmark of entrepreneurship.

Who Accepts Dirty, Poor-Paying, Dangerous Jobs?

The explanation of why some persons will accept risky jobs may in some cases be that individuals like the excitement of danger, or enjoy a reputation for courage. But most cases probably are like those described in a newspaper story about a trucker:

> Francisco Rodriguez Earns a Living Driving in Latin War Zones, [on the] 'most dangerous highway' in the world, that between Guatemala City and San Jose, Costa Rica. Mr. Rodriguez explains, 'I do it for the money, not for the excitement. And because I have to stay in business' in the face of declining demand due to the dangerous conditions.[2]

Clear evidence for the DrEf hypothesis with respect to risk is seen in the phenomenon of richer persons paying poorer persons to serve for them in the service in wartime, as for example in the Americal Civil War. (In some cases this could be viewed as a business decision based on the higher opportunity cost of the better-off person, but surely this does not explain the phenomenon completely.)

Why are many healthy native persons of working age unemployed at the same time that perhaps a couple of million foreigners illegally in the United States can find jobs, even though the illegals face such job-seeking obstacles as illegality, and lack of knowledge of the economy and culture and language? The obvious answer is that the illegals in the United States and guestworkers in West Germany will accept opportunities that native unemployed persons will not accept – 'dirty' jobs, and painful tasks such as stoop labour that natives will not do at the offered wages – because illegals are less wealthy in assets and in entitlements to transfer-payment programmes than are natives. For example:

> Sugar Growers Import Labor From West Indies to Do A 'Near Impossible' Job. Belle Glade, Fla. . . .
> The bulk of the visitors here are muscular men from the West Indies imported by local sugar growers to harvest the cane – work so grueling that even Belle Glade's mass of Haitian refugees and illegal migrants will have nothing to do with it.
> 'I don't know of any agricultural job that's more difficult than cutting sugar cane', says Ralph Alewine, a Labor Department official who oversees the importation of the 9,300 cane cutters needed in Florida's cane fields each season. 'It isn't impossible to do the work, but it's darn near impossible.'
> Indeed, no white man in 25 years has completed the six-month cane-cutting season; only a handful since World War II have tried.[3]

Reduction in Drug Use

Take it as a fact – whether it is or not factual does not matter for now – that an increase in police pressure upon drug merchants pushes up the street price of drugs, and that this leads to an increase in crime. How to explain the phenomenon? A casual explanation is ready at hand: When the price goes up, addicts need more money to get a fix, and steal to get the money. But this explanation is outside the conventional logic of economics, because 'need' is not a concept found in economic theory. And there is no substitute mode of conventional economic analysis, to my knowledge.

The hypothesis offered here provides an explanation within the domain of economic analysis. A rise in price implies a fall in wealth to the addict. A fall in wealth increases the propensity to exert effort, *ceteris paribus*, according to the Drive–Effort hypothesis. And the commission of a crime is one of the avenues into which an increased propensity to exert effort may drive the addict. Hence we have a systematic explanation of the phenomenon that does not require the term 'need' and which introduces only economic variables as r.h.s. variables.

Life Expectancy and Effort

The effects of changes in a male head-of-household's life expectancy surely are complex. Longer expected life for an adult male implies a longer retirement period and hence less wealth per future year, *ceteris-paribus*, which would imply more time and effort spent working before retirement. Longer expected life, however, also implies less chance of sudden early death in the working years of the breadwinner leaving a family 'in need', that is, without wealth. The strong *ceteris-paribus* observed relationship across nations between life expectancy and economic growth rates – a relationship which is usually interpreted as due to better health, or to improved general social conditions for which life expectancy is a proxy – leads me to guess that the extension of the retirement period dominates, and hence that more Drive and Effort are to be expected with increased length of life.

Sudden reduction in expected length of life may have a tremendous effect upon Effort, as when a writer in the midst of a book finds out that he or she has a fatal disease and redoubles effort to finish it. (Of course the effect might be the opposite, too, if the person chooses to use the remaining time as leisure.)

Fertility and Wealth

This topic surely is less substantial than most others treated here; it should be read as a flight of theoretical fancy rather than as serious analysis.

The number of children a family brings into the world may be an expression (and an indicator) of Drive, *ceteris paribus*, though admittedly it would be a task of surpassing difficulty to hold the appropriate factors constant in an empirical test of the matter. No one who has ever been a parent will doubt that children require and receive parental effort. And if people with lower wealth are in a generalized state of higher Drive, one would therefore expect them to have more children. One would expect the same conclusion from the child-quality arguments about time and wealth and consumption goods made by Becker and others.

Having children is an opportunity available almost equally to couples in various economic circumstances. Therefore, if the expenditure of at least *some* effort is a psychological *good* in itself – which sport participation demonstrates that it is, and as Leibenstein argues it is in other contexts – then there may be additional reason for people to avail themselves of the opportunity to have children if they lack other opportunities to exert effort.

Within subsistence-agricultural societies, the data show that fertility is *positively* related to wealth,[4] which seems to run against this analysis. But this positive relationship appears less clearly or even reverses as societies get richer. And average fertility tends to decline as societies become wealthier. In addition to the many other cogent explanations offered – reduced infant mortality, change in the nature of children's and parents' time allocation, and so on – a shift in values of the sort suggested by the Drive–Effort analysis may take place which may contribute to the decline in fertility.

Fertility and Opportunities for Children

To the extent that potential parents empathize with prospective children, an increase in opportunities for the children should increase the propensity to have children. And indeed, lower population density is associated with more children in the development of the American West, as is larger farm size in Poland (for a review, see Simon, 1974). In the other direction, in various bad times such as the 1930s depression, people were heard to say that they did not want to bring children into a world that promised so little.

The Size of Firms

Earlier it was said that the analysis of firms' behaviour may be usefully carried out with only a present-value framework, safely neglecting variations in work time and effort. Now that statement needs to be amended. The work time of a firm as a *collectivity* – that is, its total time expended – need not be included in the analysis. But the work time, and especially the effort, expended by the *individuals* working in the firm – decided on by them in light of their individual 'utility' frameworks – differs under various conditions, and the size of the firm may be among those conditions. Size affects employees with respect to both wealth and opportunity, and in the same direction.

Individuals often identify with organizations to which they belong, including those with which they work. For this reason, the firm's wealth might affect the Drive–Effort of the employees.[5] And the reader may agree that employees of large organizations feel a reflected sense of wealth (and power), perhaps because the employees assume that gross assets stand for net assets (and certainly there is some positive connection between these magnitudes). Employees feel that the larger firm can 'afford' expenditures on behalf of its employees that smaller firms cannot afford, including such per-quisites as thick carpets on the floor. Given this sense of wealth, the Drive–Effort hypothesis suggests less effort on the part of employees of large firms than of small ones. Of course the individual's own sense of personal opportunity within the large firm may seem greater than within the small firm, if opportunity is thought of in the fashion described in chapter 6 on monopoly and competition, which would lead in the opposite direction. Further work – and probably empirical study – would be necessary to disentangle the two effects.

Private Versus Public Operation of Economic Activities

The theory of 'privatizing' such activities as air traffic control, prisons, veterans' hospitals, and postal services in the United States and other developed countries is as stated in the section in chapter 7 on 'Effort, Economic Development, and Property Rights'. Hanke (1985) recent-ly surveyed studies of comparisons of public versus private operation in these and other sectors and found that private operation usually is much cheaper, in accord with the theory.

Franchising Versus Company Ownership

Because it is a potentiality rather than an actuality, opportunity is more difficult to measure than is wealth. Therefore, particularly welcome are Shelton's data (1967) comparing the performances of owner/managers of fast-food restaurants in a franchised chain against the performances of company managers who filled in temporarily for owner/managers in those same restaurants due to unforeseen events such as deaths. The company managers were rewarded with hefty bonuses for good performance. But a bonus captured only a *part* of the increase in profits due to a good performance, whereas owner/managers captured all of such benefit. That is, the pay-off to owner/managers was greater than the pay-off to company managers for the same amount of effort, and hence we can say that opportunity was greater for the owner/managers.

Table 8.1 shows the results, reproduced from Shelton's table, except that a restaurant whose results were distorted from a July 4th weekend was not included in the comparisons (though shown at the bottom of the table). Shelton calculated that 'the average weekly profit for all the restaurants during [company manager] supervision was only $56.81; under [the franchise owner] the profit was $271.83 . . . only two of the 29 observations where [franchise owners] were in charge showed losses; in contrast 11 of 24 cases where [company managers] were running the restaurants showed loss operations' (p. 1257). The comparison I prefer is that in 25 of the 29 sequential pair-wise comparisons possible between the two types of managers (where there were two company managers at a given operation, two comparisons were made), the franchise owner did better, while in four of the 29 the company manager did better. It should be noted that the company managers must have had more experience than most of the franchise owners, and were selected by the company for their supposed skill, whereas franchise owners were selected only on the basis of their willingness to buy and their self-selection by motivation and self-judgement of skill, and hence the comparison is biased against owners.

Table 8.1 Results of restaurant management by franchise owners and company managers

Restaurant	Type of management	Number of weeks	Average Weekly sales (dollars)	Average Weekly profit (dollars)
A	F.O.[a]	19	3,463	124.67
	C.M.	10	1,925	28.88
C	F.O.	33	2,702	86.46
	C.M.	5	2,372	−203.99
	F.O.	49	2,648	5.29
	C.M.	19	3,210	−381.99
	F.O.	6	2,581	− 77.43
D	F.O.	141	2,665	149.24
	C.M.	12	2,353	−425.89
E	F.O.	16	4,327	385.10
	C.M.	22	4,001	72.01
	F.O.	13	4,153	494.20
F	F.O.	18	3,922	−270.62
	C.M.	10	2,835	−107.73
G	C.M.	85	2,340	−102.96
	F.O.	60	2,449	115.10
	C.M.	33	2,758	− 35.85
H	F.O.	35	3,497	304.23
	C.M.	10	3,404	− 44.25
	F.O.	46	3,100	179.80
I	F.O.	28	4.030	245.83
	C.M.	17	4,612	599.56
	F.O.	59	4,790	507.74
J	F.O.	104	2,862	97.30
	C.M.	39	3,073	− 70.67
K	C.M.	60	4,034	411.46
	F.O.	21	4,479	613.62
L	F.O.	52	5,646	982.40
	C.M.	35	3,020	99.66
	F.O.	12	5,710	970.70
M	F.O.	7	4,673	570.10
	C.M.	42	2,997	−113.88
N	F.O.	26	1,353	345.01
	C.M.	23	1,066	211.06
0	F.O.	29	1,187	186.35
	C.M.	33	950	39.90
P	F.O.	27	1,027	190.77
	C.M.	35	938	53.46

Table 8.1 (Continued)

Q	F.O.	15	451	51.41
	C.M.	15	445	– 35.15
R	F.O.	40	1,778	312.92
	C.M.	64	1,791	318.79
S	F.O.	13	424	61.48
	C.M.	91	634	– 32.96
T	F.O.	59	672	30.91
	C.M.	84	660	3.30
U	F.O.	41	1,767	321.59
	C.M.	23	1,571	285.92
V	F.O.	91	1,240	208.32
	C.M.	29	1,174	93.92
B	F.O.	6	3,514	383.03
	C.M.[b]	7	8,548	700.94
	F.O.	47	4,881	307.50

[a] The abbreviation F.O. stands for franchisee-owner; C.M. indicates the restaurant was supervised by a company-employed manager. The number of weeks shows the duration of time under each type of management.

[b] This seven-week period of company management happened to include a July 4th weekend that boosted sales volume abnormally.

Table 8.1 also shows that it was not variations in sales that accounted for most of the difference, and hence the results had to derive from better cost control. Inspection of the table also reveals that a longer period as manager does not explain the superior results of the franchise owners.

These data were adduced by Shelton, in the spirit of Leibenstein, only to show that there is *possibility* for greater efficiency in business, and that this may be large relative to allocative efficiency. The data are adduced here to show that they support the *specific hypothesis* offered in this book about a supply of effort.

Professorial Tenure

The Drive–Effort hypothesis straightforwardly suggests that the obtaining of tenure should reduce the research work done by professors, because the newly-assured future income is an increase in wealth. Again, kerbstone reasoning using common-sense concepts arrives at the same conclusion. But the common-sense concepts are *ad hoc*, and they do not lead one to measure the dollar value of the tenure to assess the effect on effort quantitatively as the Drive–Effort approach does. And the fact that the same concepts – wealth, opportunity, and Drive–Effort – can be used in a wide variety of contexts instead of *ad hoc* concepts increases the 'scientificness' of the DrEf analysis, both because of the greater generality and because the concepts tie in with the rest of the structure of economic science.

Youth and Disaffection

The combination of restricted opportunity and lack of economic 'need' – that is, the presence of a high standard of living – constitutes a recipe for lack of constructive effort. It makes sense that in a time when jobs for school leavers are hard to come by, and while there is support available from the community and from the family, youths show the opposite of constructive effort – rebellion against the system, wanton attacks on persons and property, and self-destructive drug and alcohol abuse.

Personal Attributes

(1) The Drive–Effort hypothesis predicts that beautiful girls will exert less effort in school and in response to economic opportunities than will homely girls. Beauty may be thought of as wealth, because it influences the flow of future income from such sources as suitors' gifts and support by rich husbands. Once again, wealth (in the sense of command over goods in the future) seems a more precise concept here than 'need', the concept often invoked in ordinary discussion of such a phenomenon.

(2) Mental shortcomings can lead to productive effort, as Hayek tells us based on his own experience:

Alfred North Whitehead is quoted as saying that 'muddle-headedness is a condition precedent to independent thought'. That is certainly my experience. It was because I did not remember the answers that to others may have been obvious that I was often forced to think out a solution to a problem which did not exist for those who had a more orderly mind. That the existence of this sort of knowledge is not wholly unfamiliar is shown by the only half-joking description of an educated person as one who has forgotten a great deal. Such submerged memories may be quite important guides of judgment.

I am inclined to call minds of this type the 'puzzlers'. But I shall not mind if they are called the muddlers, since they certainly will often give this impression if they talk about a subject before they have painfully worked through with some degree of clarity.

Their constant difficulties, which in rare instances may be rewarded by a new insight, are due to the fact that they cannot avail themselves of the established verbal formulae or arguments which lead others smoothly and quickly to the result. But being forced to find their own way of expressing an accepted idea, they sometimes discover that the conventional formula conceals gaps or unjustified tacit presuppositions. They will be forced explicitly to answer questions which had been long effectively evaded by a plausible but ambiguous turn of phrase of an implicit but illegitimate assumption. (1960)

Relative Wealth

Brenner (1983) has constructed a motivational theory in which one's position in the wealth distribution is seen to be an index of one's chances for survival, which is seen to depend upon others' power over the individual in question. That is, if you are low in the wealth distribution you feel that many others have power over you, and therefore you struggle to raise your position in the distribution in order to reduce their power and thereby to increase your survival chances, according to Brenner.

There may be an important element of truth in this construction. Certainly it is consistent with much behaviour. And it is not inconsistent with the implicit point of view of this book, which is that a relatively low position in an unequal distribution indicates that there is opportunity to improve one's situation. If there will be equality of purchasing power no matter what one does or does not do, there is no opportunity to improve one's self in that connection.

Brenner's point of view and mine are mostly complementary, and lead to conflicting predictions only in a minority of cases. But further exploration of the meaning of relative income must be left for treatment elsewhere.

General Economic and Non-Economic Behaviour

The concepts of economics are sometimes abused by persons who suggest that economic concepts alone are sufficient to understand all human behaviour. But it is also true that application of economic concepts to situations not ordinarily thought of as subject to economic analysis can be illuminating, as I believe the following example shows.

Consider a mother and father discussing how to raise a 14-year-old son to have greater work discipline. The son is assigned a task to fix a pane of glass he and his friends broke. The son mentions a difficulty in the task, getting the glass home from the store. One of the parents offers to drive the son to the store, rather than the son going by bicycle or bus. Such an act might not only diminish the effort required in this task, but might also reduce the flow of effort in the future, because having a parent who will provide such aid certainly is an economic asset, and thereby makes a child feel richer, which would further reduce the flow of effort. (Of course other psychological forces might also affect the flow of effort in such a situation, such as camaraderie between son and parents, discouragement and helplessness at confronting what is perceived to be too formidable a task, anger at parents, and so forth. But illuminating this one aspect of the matter may help one make a better overall analysis.)

Giving Blood

Giving blood is an illuminating phenomenon because the time required for the activity is almost surely of minor importance compared to the 'effort' represented by the discomfort, the potential suffering from hepatitis, and so on. The payment is the same for all persons. Therefore, if the law permits, poor people are more likely to sell their blood than are rich people. Only a formulation that makes the increment of income relative to the person's wealth discriminates between the behaviour of the poor and the rich in this case. And the Drive–Effort formulation is quite clearly more precise here than is the concept of need.

Being Helpful

Laboratory experiments show that people are more likely to assist another when they feel that the other person's welfare is more rather than less dependent on the assistance (Berkowitz, 1978). This may be interpreted as meaning that a larger opportunity to help induces more effort than does a smaller opportunity to help, given the small level of personal cost.

Activities Undertaken for Other than Material Gain

The main ideas offered in this book were conceived while touring Italy and observing the legacy of long-ago emperors, holy beggars, martyrs, and other manner of persons not mainly motivated by the accumulation of wealth. Certainly, many of humankind's most important economic activities are undertaken for reasons other than material gain. Some great economist (Frank Knight would seem likely) has remarked that all ultimate purposes are non-economic. Therefore, if the Drive–Effort hypothesis can throw light on why individuals and groups perform some of the economic acts that are done for reasons other than personal gain, it would be a feather in the cap of the hypothesis.

Earlier, the aim of these chapters was stated as better understanding of *economic* behaviour, and the Drive–Effort Measure is defined in a manner as is intended to do that. But if we now wish to consider behaviour other than 'economic' – that is, behaviour whose main effects are other than the economic actor's material well-being – the Drive–Effort Measure must be redefined. It is hoped that a more general formulation of the same general idea also will have some analytic power.

Let us replace the term 'wealth' with the term 'standing'; the term 'endowment' would have the correct connotation to economists, but to non-economists it suggests that the person received an inheritance, whereas 'standing' is meant to imply the amount of personal honour, or community reputation, or piety in the eyes of religious community or self, or formal status in a hierarchy, or any other attribute that a person may value, given the time, the place, and the person's own scale of values. And it is then assumed that Drive–Effort is the same sort of function as set out earlier in (4.1) except that it is now specified as

$$\text{Drive–Effort Measure} = b\left(\frac{S_{n+1} - S_n}{S_n}\right) \text{where } S = \text{standing.} \quad (8.1)$$

Let us now offer some speculations in light of this expanded hypothesis:

(1)   All else equal, a non-respected person such as an ex-criminal may, when asked, be more likely than a respected citizen to perform a community service, because the former has lower standing (smaller 'wealth') with respect to honour by the community.

(2)   A person thought of by community and self as a great sinner would be more likely to exhibit a dramatic conversion to piety and salvation than would a person previously regarded as among the righteous.

(3)   In times when courtly titles were important, a person with no title – say a successful merchant – would pay more for a given title than would a lower noble with the same economic position.

(4)   The newly-rich, who therefore lack the reputation of being rich, seem more willing to purchase the conspicuous trappings of wealth than are people of 'old money'. So marketers think, anyway.

Socially Productive Leisure of the Rich?

When we consider the situation of the wealthy, another – and entirely different – view of effort enters the picture, if we assume that *some* expenditure of effort and the associated energy is a good in itself. And it does seem reasonable, from watching young children at play, or a young puppy frolicking with a ball or chasing its tail, or watching sailors penned up on a ship at sea endlessly wandering around, or any of us when we cannot as usual be out and doing and instead suffer 'cabin fever', that just doing things is often a positive good in itself. If we assume that a certain given amount of activity will be forthcoming, the amount of a person's wealth will influence the *choice* of activities, and will result in producing fewer activities whose pay-off is in money and more activities whose pay-off is in honour, sex, and other desired aspects of life, compared to less wealthy persons.

For centuries, many have believed that wealth benefits society by freeing people from working for money so that they might work at other socially-useful activities. Hayek (1960, p. 127) puts this classical theme as follows: 'There must be, in other words, a tolerance for the existence of a group of idle rich – idle not in the sense that they do nothing useful but in the sense that their aims are not entirely governed by considerations of material gain.' He cites such 'gentleman-scholars' of the nineteenth century as Darwin, Macaulay, Grote, Lubbock, Motley, Henry Adams, Tocqueville, and Schliemann. And he thinks it better that private wealth should act at second hand to make possible such patronized scholars as Karl Marx than that government employment in universities and elsewhere should be the sole means of their support (p. 128).

Perhaps so. But one might also speculate that in rich countries inequalities of income produced by inherited wealth are not necessary to make large amounts of leisure time possible for individuals. A very large proportion of persons in the United States could cut their incomes in half without affecting basic subsistence. If they did so by reducing their required work time by that proportion, they would have plenty of leisure necessary to produce the sort of scholarly and scientific work envisioned by Hayek. Furthermore, being involved in the world's work on a day-to-day basis probably has the salutary effect of bringing important problems to a person's notice. And the supply of problems must surely be the most important input to a first-class thinker's output.

When making an assessment of this matter on balance, one might also keep in mind Bishop Berkeley's (1735) question: 'Whether every man who had money enough would not be a gentleman? And whether a nation of gentlemen would not be a wretched nation?' composed mainly of profligates and wastrels rather than of socially productive persons.

Bold Projects and Grand Creation

Aside from the previous section, the book has focused on the input of effort into economic and non-economic activity without attending to various kinds of outputs. Let us turn for a moment to a special kind of output – the great achievements of humankind whether in engineering, art, science, politics, or even war. Let us ask about the conditions under which an individual will strive towards, and perhaps attain, such a great achievement.

Wealth is the complicating element. On the one hand, the DrEf formulation asserts that greater wealth, *ceteris paribus*, implies less effort and hence less achievement. On the other hand, cathedrals are not built without wealth, and Nobel prize winners are more likely to do their work in rich countries than in poor ones. An acceptable discussion of the preconditions for great achievements must resolve this apparent contradiction.

A resolution may be found in two distinctions: between individual projects and group projects, and between the *possession* of wealth as a personal asset, and *access* to wealth as a tool to be used in grand creations. Concerning the former distinction, the DrEf hypothesis refers to the motivation and activity of individuals rather than groups, and therefore we must limit the discussion here to projects in which the decision to 'go for it' is made by the same individual who exerts the main effort and who expects the main fruits of the achievement, such as painting or the study of DNA or exploration of the Americas, and not to building pyramids in which case the order is given by a Pharaoh and the effort is made by managers and slaves.

Great achievements usually require, in addition to Drive and Effort, capital of various kinds: a stock of knowledge held by the civilization, a quantum of human capital measured in the numbers and in the 'quality' of persons available to co-operate in the project, physical capital in the form of existing equipment and structures, and financial capital for mobilizing the human and physical capital. A wealthy and populous society has more of these ingredients than does a poor and small society. An individual who will strive for a great achievement need not own the necessary physical or financial capital; it can sometimes be borrowed, or obtained by patronage or grant. This suggests that the appropriate conditions for a great achievement are: first, the existence of the necessary knowledge and capital within the society that the potential creator lives in or moves to; second, the absence of large wealth in the personal endowment of the potential creator; third, the possession by the potential creator of sufficient education to complement his or her 'natural' talent, education which can usually be best obtained in a wealthy society; and fourth, opportunity to make a great achievement in a field open to the potential creator. More must be said about this fourth precondition.

It would seem that great achievements are more likely to occur when the potential creator (or group) perceives that great achievement is possible. The best example I can find unfortunately pertains to group achievement rather than to the individual achievement with which this book deals, but the point should not be confused thereby. When the great wave of cathedral building began sometime at the beginning of this millennium, the available knowledge and capital made it possible for a creator to dream of (as Gimpel, 1976, put it) a 'world record' cathedral in terms of height, and then another and another. At some point, the potential for such advances was reduced as the stock of unused knowledge was depleted, and this constraint – in addition to other developments in the years around the time of the Black Death – may well have checked the wave of great cathedral building. Similarly, the wave of railroad building in the United States, together with the wave of inventions that accompanied it, largely came to an end when great railroad achievements had been completed for the largest existing markets.

The fact that immigrants from poorer countries have so often made great achievements surely fits in here, but to pursue the topic would be both speculative and digressive.

Notes

1   See Hicks (1935/1952).
2   *Wall Street Journal*, 16 December 1983, p. 1.

3   *Wall Street Journal*, 3 January 1985, p. 1.
4   For example, see: Stys (1957), Simon (1974); see Simon (1977, Part II), for a review.
5   The reader may note that the notion of wealth used here is total wealth of the collectivity, whereas in another application – family size – wealth per person is the concept used. There need not be any contradiction here, since we are dealing with the individual's perceptions. And sometimes one focuses on the size of an entire entity, and sometimes on the size of its parts. In some cases an individual may focus on both, and there may be opposing effects, in which case the analysis would not be simple. But for now we may put aside this matter.

9

Summary, Policy Implications, and Discussion

Summary

Necessity and opportunity evoke those aspects of economic behaviour
that require effort, drive, time, and sacrifice. This book analyses the
carrot of opportunity together with the stick of the lack of wealth.
Economists have done well in analysing the carrot but poorly in
analysing the stick. And economics has not tried at all to analyse their
joint effect when presented in combination – as they always are.
Hopefully this book improves on this situation.

Straightforward net-present-value profit-maximization analysis
suffices for the study of the behaviour of firms under most conditions.
Becker's theory of time allocation supplements profit maximization
for the study of individuals' behaviour. But the expenditure of time in
work, with the consequent loss of leisure, is not the only personal
good expended in order to obtain purchasing power. Other goods
expended include the absorption of pain due to fatigue, loss of
reputation and honour, and forgone serenity. For the purposes of
the analysis offered in this book, these and other related factors are
classed together and referred to as Effort, and the impulse to expend
them is here referred to as Drive.

The analysis postulates that the strength of Drive experienced, and
the amount of Effort expended, may be modelled as the difference
between opportunity and wealth, relative to wealth. This Drive–
Effort function may be seen as a close intellectual relative (even as the
transformation) of the logarithmic (Benthamic) marginal utility
function, and of the Weber–Fechner law of psychophysics.

The Drive–Effort Measure as defined here is offered as a precise and unambiguous definition of the concept of incentive, a concept which is used in economics frequently but without clear specification.

After the introduction in chapter 1, chapters 2–4 set the topic in the context of previous thinking, state the Drive–Effort (DrEf) concept formally, and discuss how it may be measured.

Data that cast light upon the relationship of individual effort to wealth are presented in chapter 5; they mostly confirm the inverse function hypothesized. Tests of the hypothesis are also suggested in chapter 5. There then follows an extended analysis in chapter 6 of the difference in effort to be expected in duopoly versus monopoly, based on the Drive–Effort hypothesis. Applications of the analysis to such diverse macro-phenomena as the rise and decline of nations, and the origin of economic development in the temperate climes rather than in the tropics or arctic regions, are presented in chapter 7. Micro applications, such as the individual's decision about whether to accept overtime work, are discussed in chapter 8.

Policy Implications

If effort affects economic performance, and the amount of effort depends upon the circumstances – as defined by the Drive–Effort Measure – one naturally wonders: What can policymakers and economists do to increase effort?

The first principle would seem to be: above all, do no harm. The likeliest cause of well-intended harm is selectively giving special incentives to those persons or groups that seem to need energizing. Such special incentives almost surely lead to perverse twists in the economy, and induce people to search for subsidy situations instead of for productive economic opportunities, outcomes far worse than the conditions the incentives are intended to correct.

The corollary of the first principle is that society should reduce the regulations and barriers which constrain potential creators of enterprises and innovations. If one must get permission from a wide variety of agencies, and file a long series of complex environmental impact statements, and worry that after building a plant and hiring workers the plant cannot be closed and the workers let go if conditions require, and on and on and on, then potential entrepreneurs will be less likely to take big risks in putting a satellite in space, or mining the sea, or building a nuclear fusion plant. Instead, individuals and entrepreneurial firms will turn to financial adventuring such as selling tax shelters and fighting to take over existing firms. Already few enough are the persons with sufficient stars in their eyes and iron in their souls to dream big dreams of accomplishing what people never before have done. The society should encourage rather than discourage such people by making the game worth the candle, and by freeing them up to be able to reach for the main chance. Such advancement of freedom is the sound economics of the human spirit, and the workable theory of economic development.

The liberty to make a deal with whomever one likes, any place in the world, is a key aspect of freedom; this conclusion follows from the discussion on page 148 about the relationship of the size of the market to opportunity. The other side of the same coin is that firms should not be protected against the competition of domestic or foreign competitors who want to make deals. This conclusion implies that there should be no tariff walls, no protection for infant industries, and no social opprobrium for buying abroad.

The Drive–Effort hypothesis suggests that in addition to their bad side, income inequalities have advantages because they imply both lower wealth and higher opportunity for some individuals or groups than would the same total amount of income divided equally. So if, for example, one nation forges ahead technologically for a while, there is a positive effect on effort by the laggard countries through the Drive–Effort mechanism, in addition to the new technology which the backward nations can exploit.

Increased immigration into advanced countries is shown to have a beneficial effect by way of the Drive–Effort hypothesis, because economic immigrants are likely to have less wealth than do natives of the country of immigration; hence the immigrants will undertake opportunities that natives will not. This effect goes in the same direction as the net of other effects of immigrants (see Simon, forthcoming).

All this adds up to a relatively open economy, of course, in accord with the view of Adam Smith and the other Scottish and English classical economists; it is also the view of a wide variety of economists who are not all found in Chicago or 'Austria.' It also adds up to an open *society* in the spirit of the classical liberals from the time at least of Mandeville, on down to Popper and Hayek.

Implicit in many schemes for reforming societies and for making them less 'aggressive' or 'savage' or 'competitive' is the idea that individuals can be motivated to work hard by ideals 'higher' than the immediate urge to acquire purchasing power. No logical argument disproves this idea. And under some circumstances – usually emergencies such as war – the idea may be sound. But data presented in chapter 5, together with recent experiences in China and other socialist countries, suggest that these schemes will not be successful in the long run. This being so, the DrEf Measure takes on added importance as a useful way of thinking about the motivation of economic activity.

Discussion

(1) Too much explanatory power should not be claimed for the DrEf hypothesis, of course. For example, the DrEf hypothesis may explain why Venice and Genoa – unlike other cities – exerted the enormous efforts that they did to become the leading trade cities that they were; they had the geographic opportunity. But that Venice won and Genoa lost in the struggle for pre-eminence between them surely happened because of other historical and chance factors rather than because of their relative opportunities and wealth.[1]

(2) One may wonder, in light of the variety of illustrations offered here in support of the Drive–Effort hypothesis: Is the central proposition so broad that it can be made to fit *any* human situation? If so, the hypothesis would be worthless because of being tautologous. There are many situations, however, to which the Drive–Effort hypothesis does *not* apply – the Arab-Israeli wars, most behaviour of parents toward children and vice versa, gazing in rapture at a sunset.

(3) The aim of the Drive–Effort analysis is *not* to reconceptualize standard economics. Rather, the aim is to bring a key economic variable into the ambit of standard theory. The closest analogy is Hicks and then Becker bringing time within that ambit along with physical inputs to the production process. The bringing-in of education by Schultz, and of information by Hayek and Stigler, also

are analogous. I emphasize this point because there may be a tendency to wonder whether the Drive–Effort hypothesis is simply a matter of re-organizing well-established entities in new ways; it is not.

One might also wonder whether it is necessary or useful to bother enlarging the framework for this purpose, or whether economics has done well enough without it in the past and therefore can continue to do without it. As to such an analysis being necessary, a treatment of effort seems needed for understanding the workings of business and other economic institutions, because effort is well recognized in the workplace as being crucial. One only needs read a newspaper for a few days with an eye open to this factor to find plenty of examples of the operation of effort and its related elements. Here are a few recent examples to add to the many given earlier:

(a) A business journalist who was fired from his job gives the following advice to others who are fired:

> Be eager to relocate. Don't be so provincial as to think the world revolves around New York, Los Angeles, Chicago or your home town. The work and the living can be excellent almost anywhere, if you go with the right attitude.
>
> Most of all, don't give up. Keep trying. Stay motivated, no matter what. Remember that many of us have gone through the hell you are going through. Keep plugging and in time the light at the end of the tunnel will be not that of an oncoming train but of a new opportunity.
>
> (Henney, 1982)

'Don't give up. Keep trying. Stay motivated.' All are synonyms for continuing to exert effort. Effort is a variable, he is saying, and the amount of effort exerted matters.

(b) A consultant advises that a wage increase may elicit an increase in productivity that will more than pay for the wage increase, citing not only the legendary five-dollar-a-day Ford example but also recent industrial experience.

> Consider a program at the Muskegon Piston Ring Co., largest manufacturer of piston rings in the world.
>
> In 1975 the automotive original equipment division at the Muskegon plant was losing $1 million a year and

operating at 40% of capacity. With the cooperation of the union, the company decided to raise both the base pay and the production requirements for employees. The company reversed its financial position to a $1 million annual profit. Plant equipment was operating at 80%, and take-home pay rose by 70 cents an hour.

Or consider Eclipse, Inc., a Rockford, Ill.-based manufacturer of industrial heating equipment, with some 650 employees. In 1978 employee turnover was 95% per year, daily absenteeism was running at about 10% and there had been a five-year slide in earnings.

The company decided to offer wage incentives based on individual and overal company performance, and scheduled merit reviews of all employees, including supervisors. Wages rose by 34% over three years, employee turnover was reduced to 20% per year and absenteeism to less than 3%. Meanwhile shipping volume per employee rose 65 per cent and company profits have jumped 600%.

In 1960, Patrick Cudahy Inc., the packing firm, broke off negotiations with the Amalgamated Meat Cutters & Butchers Union over a 17-cent per hour increase, and announced it was closing its plant because of continued high losses. The union later accepted a management offer for a 37-cent per hour base rate increase, coupled with higher requirements for employee output and other changes in work methods. The company afterward realized the highest profit in its history. (Patton, 1982)

The writer is not suggesting that productivity automatically rises when wages go up, but rather that workers will make more effort and therefore produce more output if they find that they must do so in order to obtain higher wages or continued employment.

This latter quotation is particularly relevant because it makes clear that the increase in productivity arises from greater intensity of effort within the same number of work hours, rather than from an increase in work time which might be dealt with by recourse to Becker's allocation-of-time analysis or some extension of it.

(c) The harder times (for example, reduced wealth) in the late 1970s and the early 1980s affected labour's willingness to exert more effort (called 'productivity' here):

> Ten – even five – years ago, anyone who mentioned 'capital formation' or 'productivity' to a labor leader was dismissed as a 'tool of the bosses'. At best such matters were considered none of the union's business and 'what management is being paid for'. By now, few inside or outside union ranks would deny that the worker's welfare depends on capital formation and productivity – even in the very short run. The two largely determine how many jobs there can be, how secure they can be and how well paid they can be. (Drucker, 1982)

Drucker argues that this development reduces the importance of unions, certainly an important matter for effort analysis to help explain.

(d) Harder times also increase the Drive of business executives to exert the Effort to carry out painful decisions such as shutting down plants.

> In 1979, General Tire & Rubber Co. decided that its big plant in Akron, a multistory operation for manufacturing bias-ply truck tires, was obsolete. The company, however, promised to try to replace it with a modern plant if workers would make concessions to cut labor costs. The employees' union agreed. But last March, in what M. G. O'Neil, chairman and president, called 'the most difficult and painful announcement I have ever made', the company said it would close the 67-year-old plant.[2]

The terms 'trying', and 'difficult and painful', in the second and last sentences in the quotation refer to Drive–Effort.

(e) In conventional analysis, it seems out of joint with the times when a person starts a business during a recession. But recession apparently raises the rate of new business starts in some fields. Dun and Bradstreet reported that in the depressed second quarter of 1982, 'there was a rise of almost 7 per cent in new services, including increases for laundries, advertising agencies and data-processing companies though entry into construction and mining fell'.[3] Entrepreneurship requires effort to a high degree, including battling against fearful uncertainty and frightening personal risk. It is in accord with the Drive–Effort hypothesis that when people's sense of wealth declines due to economic downturn, they should then be more willing to exert the effort to start new businesses.

(f) Avoiding waste and using inputs efficiently requires effort. And the Drive–Effort hypothesis suggests that those who are poorer in a resource will exert more effort to conserve it. It is to be expected that with respect to oil and energy, 'the country that has adjusted the most is Japan, which began from the most energy-spare base. In 1973, Japan used 57 per cent as much energy for every unit of G.N.P. as the United States. By 1980, it used only 43 per cent.' (Yergin, 1982)

(g) Decreased wealth due to increased competition can spur wholly new effort-intensive activities. The medical profession is a recent case in point. Here is an example:

> Reports indicate that many doctors are paying more attention to pleasing their patients. The busy Mayo Clinic in Rochester, Minn. . . . has placed a 'patient's representative' in its lobby to hear complaints. One reason, says Mark Brataas, a clinic administrator, is the need for doctors to 'market' themselves in the face of today's growing competition from increasing numbers of health plans and doctors.   (Cohn, 1985)

One can deny the need for theoretical attention to variations in effort only if one dismisses anecdotal and introspective reports of effort variation as being too 'soft' to be entered into evidence in the discourse of economic theory. In my view, to simply dismiss such reports as being unsystematic, without developing a superior replacement, is simply sticking one's head in the sand for the sake of 'convenience', that is, for the sake of avoiding the very sort of effort that this book is about.

Notes

1 'Over the long run, the outcome of Venetian-Genoese rivalry was not to depend on superiority in seamanship or naval operations; after 1270,

Venice had no such superiority. It was decided by their relative skill in arts of another order – those of social organization, in which the Genoese and the Venetians had very different talents' (Lane, 1973, pp. 84–5).

2 *Wall Street Journal*, 15 October 1982, p. 29.
3 *Wall Street Journal*, 30 September 1982, p. 1.

References

Adler, Mortimer J., et al., *The Works of the Mind* (Chicago: University of Chicago Press, 1947).

Arenson, Karen W. 'On the Frontier of a New Economics', *The New York Times*, 31 October, 1982, section 3, p. 1.

Arrow, Kenneth J., *The Limits of Organization* (New York: Norton, 1974).

Bain, Joe S., *Barriers to New Competition* (Cambridge, Mass.: Harvard University Press, 1956).

Baldamus, W., 'The Relationship Between Wage and Effort', *Journal of Industrial Economics*, 1957, pp. 192–201.

Barnes, Carl B., 'The Partial Effect of Income on Suicide Is Always Negative', *American Journal of Sociology*, 1974.

Barnes, William F., 'Job Search Models, the Duration of Unemployment, and the Asking Wage: Some Empirical Evidence', *The Journal of Human Resources*, vol. x, no. 2, pp. 230–40.

Barnett, Harold J. and Morse, Chandler, *Scarcity and Growth: The Economics of Natural Resource Availability* (Baltimore: Johns Hopkins, 1963).

Bauer, Peter T., *Dissent on Development* (London: Weidenfeld and Nicholson, 1976).

Bauer, Peter T., *Equality, the Third World and Economic Delusion* (London and Cambridge, Mass.: Harvard University Press, 1981.)

Bauer, Peter T., *Reality and Rhetoric*, (Cambridge, Mass.: Harvard University Press, 1984).

Baumol, William J., 'Contestable Markets: An Uprising in the Theory of Industry Structure', *American Economic Review*, 72, March 1982, pp. 1–15.

Becker, Gary S., 'A Theory of the Allocation of Time', *Economic Journal*, 75, September 1965, pp. 493–517.

Becker, Gary S., *The Economic Approach to Human Behavior* (Chicago: University of Chicago Press, 1976).

Becker, Gary S., 'Specialized Human Capital, the Allocation of Effort, and Differences in Earnings and Time Allocation of Married Men and Women', mimeo, April 1983.

Becker, Gary S. and Michael, 'On the Theory of Consumer Behavior', *Swedish Journal of Economics*, vol. 75, 1973, pp. 378–95. Reprinted in Becker, 1976.

Bell, Daniel, *The Coming of Post-Industrial Society* (New York: Basic Books, 1973/1976).

Bell, Daniel, *The Cultural Contradictions of Capitalism* (New York: Basic Books, 1976).

Berkeley, Bishop, *The Querist*, 1735, quoted by George J. Stigler and Claire Friedland in calendar.

Berkowitz, Leonard, 'Decreased helpfulness with increased group size through lessening the effects of the needy individual's dependency', *Journal of Personality*, 46, 1978, pp. 299–310.

Billsborrow, Richard E., 'Dependency Rates and Aggregate Savings Rates Revisited: Corrections, Further Analysis, and Recommendations for the Future', in J. Simon and J. DaVanzo, eds, *Research in Population Economics* (Greenwich: JAI Press, 1980).

Boserup, Ester, *The Conditions of Agricultural Growth* (London: George Allen and Unwin, 1965).

Boulding, Kenneth E., *Conflict and Defense* (New York: Harper, 1962).

Boulding, Kenneth E., *Economics as a Science* (New York: McGraw-Hill, 1977).

Bowen, William and Finegan, T. Aldrich, *The Economics of Labor Force Participation* (Princeton, NJ: Princeton University Press, 1969).

Bradburn, N. M. and Caplovitz David, *Reports of Happiness* (Chicago: Aldine, 1965).

Breer, Paul E. and Locke, Edwin A., *A Task Experience as a Source of Attitudes* (Homewood, Ill.: The Dorsey Press, 1965).

Brenner, Rueven, *History – The Human Gamble* (Chicago: University of Chicago Press, 1983).

Briggs, Asa, *A Social History of England* (New York: The Viking Press, 1984).

Brown, Charles, Gilroy, Curtis and Kohen, Andres, 'The Effect of the Minimum Wage on Employment and Unemployment', *The Journal of Economic Literature*, vol. xx, no. 2, June 1982, pp. 489–90.

Buchanan, James M., *What Should Economists Do?* (Indianapolis: Liberty Press, 1979).

Burtless, Gary and Greenberg, David, 'Measuring the Impact of NIT Experiments on Work Effort', *Industrial and Labor Relations Review*, vol. 36, no. 4, July 1983, pp. 592–605.

Burtless, Gary and Greenberg, David, 'Inappropriate Comparisons as a

Basis for Policy: Two Recent Examples from the Social Experiments', *Journal of Public Policy*, August 1983, pp. 381–99.

Butterfield, Fox, *China: Alive in the Bitter Sea* (New York: Bantam Books, 1982).

Cable, John and FitzRoy, Felix, 'Productive Efficiency, Incentives and Employee Participation: Some Preliminary Results for West Germany', *Kyklos*, vol. 33, 1980, pp. 100–21.

Cahan, Abraham, *The Rise of David Levinsky* (New York, Harper and Row, 1917/1960).

Carter, Sir Charles, 'Conditions for the Successful Use of Science', *Science*, vol.219, March 18, 1983.

Carey, Alex, 'The Hawthorne Studies: A Radical Criticism', *American Sociological Review*, 32, June 1967, pp. 403–47.

Caves, R.E. and Porter M. E., 'From Entry Barriers to Mobility Barriers: Conjectural Decisions and Contrived Deterrence to New Competition', *Quarterly Journal of Economics*, vol. 91, no.2, 1977, pp. 241–61.

Chayanov, A. V., *The Theory of Peasant Economy*, D. Thorner et al., eds (Homewood: Irwin, 1923/1966).

Childe, Gordon, *What Happened in History* (Baltimore: Penguin Books, 1942).

Cipolla, Carlos, *The Economic Decline of Empires* (London: Methuen, 1970), p. 6.

Clark, Colin, *Conditions of Economic Progress*, 3rd edn (New York: Macmillan, 1957).

Clark, Ronald W., *Einstein: The Life and Times* (New York, 1971).

Clough, Shepard B., *The Rise and Fall of Civilization* (New York, Columbia University Press, 1951/1957).

Cohn, Victor, 'Sometimes, They Listen', *Washington Post*, 23 January 1985, Medical Section, p. 8.

Cournot, Augustin, *Research in the Mathematical Principles of the Theory of Wealth* (Homewood: Irwin, 1838/1963).

Creel, H. G., *Chinese Thought: From Confucius to Mao Tse-Tung* (New York: The New American Library, 1953).

Cyert, R. M. and DeGroot, M.H., 'Bayesian Analysis and Duopoly Theory', *Journal of Political Economy*, September–October 1970, pp. 1168–84.

Cyert, R. M. and DeGroot, M.H., 'Multi-Period Decision Models with Alternating Choice as a Solution to the Duopoly Problem', *Quarterly Journal of Economics*, August 1970, pp. 410–29.

Cyert, R. M., Feigenbaum, E.A. and March, J. G., 'Models in a Behavioral Theory of the Firm', *Behavioral Science*, April 1959, pp. 81–95.

Davenport, Herbert J., *The Economics of Enterprise* (New York: Augustus M. Kelley, 1913/1968).

De Allesi, Louis, 'Property Rights, Transaction Costs, and X-Efficiency: An Essay in Economic Theory', *The American Economic Review*, March 1983, pp. 64–81.

Drucker, Peter F., 'Are Unions Becoming Irrelevant?', *Wall Street Journal*, September 22 1982, p. 32.

Einstein, Albert, *Ideas and Opinions* (New York: Bonanza Books, 1954).

Elliot, J. H., *The Old World and the New (1492–1650)* (Cambridge: Cambridge University Press, 1970).

Farr, James L., 'Incentive Schedules, Productivity, and Satisfaction in Work Groups: A Laboratory Study', *Organizational Behavior and Human Performance*, 17, 1976, p. 159.

Feldstein, Martin, 'Social Security, Induced Retirement, and Aggregate Capital Accumulation', *Journal of Political Economy*, vol. 82, no. 5, September–October 1974, pp. 905–26.

Fellner, William, *Competition Among the Few* (New York: Knopf, 1949).

Ferguson, Charles E. and Pfouts, Ralph W., 'Learning and Expectation in Dynamic Duopoly Behavior', *Behavioral Science*, April 1962, pp. 223–37.

Ferrier, David, *The Functions of the Brain* (New York: Putnam, 1886).

Ferris, Richard J., 'You Can't Sell the Sizzle Without the Steak', *United Airlines Magazine*, December 1982.

Filer, Randall, 'The Downturn in Productivity Growth: A New Look at Its Nature and Causes', in Shlomo Maital and Noah Meltz, eds, *Lagging Productivity Growth: Causes and Remedies* (Cambridge, Mass.: Ballinger, 1979).

Filer, Randall K., 'The Influence of Affective Human Capital on the Wage Equation', *Research in Labor Economics*, 4, 1981, pp. 367–416.

Filer, Randall K., 'Joint Estimates of the Supply of Labor Hours and the Intensity of Work Effort', xerox, May 1986.

Filer, Randall K., 'People and Productivity: Effort Supply as Viewed by Economists and Psychologists', in B. Gilad and S. Kaish, eds, *Handbook of Behavioral Economics* (Greenwich, Connecticut: JAI Press, forthcoming).

Fisher, Allan George Barnard, *The Clash of Progress and Security* (London, Macmillan, 1935. Reprinted A. M. Kelley, 1966).

Fisher, Irving, *The Theory of Interest* (New York: Macmillan, 1930).

Franke, H.F. and Kaul, J.D., 'The Hawthorne Experiments: First Statistical Interpretation', *American Sociological Review*, 43, 1978, pp. 623–43.

Franke, Richard H., 'Worker Productivity at Hawthorne', *American Sociological Review*, December 1980, pp. 1006–27.

Freedman, Ronald, 'The Sociology of Human Fertility', *Current Sociology*, vol. 11–12, 1961–1962, pp. 35–121.

Friedman, James, 'Reaction Functions and the Theory of Duopoly', *Review of Economic Studies*, July 1968, pp. 257–72.

Friedman, James, 'On Experimental Research in Oligopoly', *Review of Economic Studies*, October 1969, pp. 399–416.

Friedman, Milton and Friedman, Rose, *Free to Choose* (New York: Avon Books, 1980).

Galanter, E. H., quoted in S. S. Stevens, 'Measurement, Psychophysics, and Utility', in C. W. Churchman and P. Ratoosh, eds, *Measurement: Definitions and Theories* (New York: Wiley, 1959), chapter 2.

Gayer, David, 'The Effects of Wages, Unearned Income and Taxes on the Supply of Labor', mimeo, World Institute, Jerusalem, 1974.

Gilboy, Elizabeth W., 'Demand Curves by Personal Estimate', *Quarterly Journal of Economics*, vol. 46, 1931, pp. 376–84.

Gilder, George, *Wealth and Poverty* (New York: Basic Books, 1984).

Gimpel, Jean, *The Medieval Machine* (New York: Penguin, 1976).

Glaser, Daniel and Rice, Kent, 'Crime, Age and Employment', *American Sociological Review*, October 1959, pp. 679–86.

Gronau, Reuben, 'The Allocation of Time of the Israeli Married Women', mimeo, Falk Institute, November 1974.

Gurin, G., et al., *Tabular Supplement to Americans View their Mental Health*, Ann Arbor, Survey Research Center, 1960.

Guthrie, Harold W., 'Who Moonlights and Why?', *Illinois Business Review*, 1965, pp. 6–8.

Guthrie, Harold W., 'Some Explanations of Moonlighting', Business and Economic Sections, *Proceedings of the American Statistical Association*, 1966.

Hagen, Everett E., *On the Theory of Social Change* (Howard, Ill.: Dorsey, 1962).

Hagen, Everett E., *The Economics of Development*, rev. edn (Homewood: Irwin, 1975).

Halberstam, David, 'Can We Rise to the Japanese Challenge?', *Parade Magazine*, pp. 4–7.

Hall, Robert E., 'Employment Fluctuations and Wage Rigidity', *Brookings Papers on Economic Activity*, vol. 1, 1980, pp. 91–123.

Hamermesh, Daniel S., 'Incentives for the Homogenization of Time Use', Working Paper no. 1397, National Bureau of Economic Research, Inc., July 1984.

Hamermesh, Daniel S. and Rees, Albert, *The Economics of Work and Pay*, 3rd edn (New York: Harper and Row, 1984).

Hanke, Steve H., 'Privatization: Theory, Evidence, and Implementation', in C. Lowell Harriss, ed., *Control of Federal Spending* (New York: The Academy of Political Science, 1985).

Harsanyi, John C., 'Games with Incomplete Information Played by 'Bayesian' Players, I–III', *Management Science*, November 1967, pp. 159–82, and subsequent issues.

Hayami, Yujiro and Ruttan, Vernon W., *Agricultural Development: An International Perspective* (Baltimore: Johns Hopkins Press, 1971).

Hayek, Friedrich A., *Individualism and Economic Order* (London: Routledge and Kegan Paul, 1949).

Hayek, Friedrich A., *The Counter-Revolution of Science* (Indianapolis: Liberty Press, 1952/1979).

Hayek, Friedrich A., *The Constitution of Liberty* (Chicago, University of Chicago Press, 1960).

Hayek, Friedrich A., Personal Communication, 22 March 1981.

Henney, Tim H., 'Canned Advice for the Newly Fired Executive', *Wall Street Journal*, 29 October 1982, p. 18.

Henry, Andrew F. and Short, James F., Jr., *Suicide and Homicide* (Glencoe, Ill.: The Free Press, 1954).

Hicks, John R., 'Annual Survey of Economic Theory: The Theory of Monopoly', *Econometrica*, iii, 1935, pp. 1–20. Reprinted in George F. Stigler and Kenneth Boulding, eds, *Readings in Price Theory* (Homewood: Irwin, 1952).

Hicks, John R., *The Theory of Wages* (London: Macmillan, 1932/1963).

Hill, C. Russell, 'Education, Health and Family Size as Determinants of Labor Market Activity for the Poor and Nonpoor', *Demography*, August 1971, vol.8, no.3, pp. 379–88.

Hill, Peter, J., 'Relative Skill and Income Levels of Native and Foreign Born Workers in the United States', *Explorations in Economic History*, vol. 12, 1975, pp. 47–60.

Hirschman, Albert O., *The Strategy of Economic Development* (New Haven: Yale University Press, 1958).

Hirschman, Albert O., *Exit, Voice and Loyalty* (Cambridge, Mass.: Harvard University Press, 1970).

Hodges, Lloyd Curry, *Clothing and Race: An Examination of the Effects of Race on Consumption*, Ph.D. Thesis (University of Illinois, 1982).

Hoelterhoff, Manuela, 'Brandel's History: The Way the World Used to Work', Review of F. Brandel, *The Structure of Everyday Life, Wall Street Journal*, 15 June 1982, p. 24.

Hofstadter, Douglas R., *Godel, Escher, Back: an Eternal Golden Braid* (New York: Random House, 1979).

Holton, Gerald, *Thematic Origins of Scientific Thought* (Cambridge, Mass.: Harvard University Press, 1973).

Hoselitz, Bert F., 'Theories Of Stages Of Economic Growth', chapter vi of Bert F. Hoselitz, ed., *Theories Of Economic Growth*, (New York: The Free Press, 1960).

Hume, David, *Political Essays* (New York: Library of Liberal Arts, Bobbs-Merrill Co., 1953), p. 135.

Hutchison, T. W., *Knowledge and Ignorance in Economics* (Chicago: University of Chicago Press, 1977).

Inkeles, Alex and Smith, David H., *Becoming Modern: Individual Change in Six Developing Countries* (Cambridge, Mass.: Harvard University Press, 1974).

James, William, *Psychology* (New York: Fawcett Publications, Inc., 1890/1963).

The Jerusalem Post, 'Record Number of Unemployed Refuse Job Offers', 23–29 January 1983.

Johnson, D. Gale, 'Agriculture in the Centrally Planned Economies', *American Journal of Agricultural Economics*, December 1982, pp. 845–53.

Johnson, Harry G., 'National Styles in Economic Research: The United States, the United Kingdom, Canada, and Various European Countries', *Daedalus*, vol. 102, no. 2 Spring 1973, pp. 65–74.

Jones, Eric L., *The European Miracle*, (Cambridge: Cambridge University Press, 1981).

Kahneman, Daniel, *Attention and Effort*, (Englewood Cliffs, NJ: Prentice-Hall, 1973).

Kasper, Hirschel, 'The Asking Price of Labor and the Duration of Unemployment', *The Review of Economics and Statistics*, xlix, May 1967, pp. 165–72.

Katona, George B. and Zahn, Ernest, *Aspirations and Affluence*, (New York: McGraw-Hill, 1971).

Kilbridge, Maurice D., 'Statistical Indicators of the Continuing Effectiveness of Wage Incentive Applications', *Journal of Industrial Economics*, 1960, pp. 83–97.

Killingsworth, Mark. R., *Labor Supply* (New York: Cambridge University Press, 1983).

Kindleberger, Charles P., *Economic Development* (New York: McGraw-Hill, 2nd edn, 1965).

King, Sandra L., 'Incentive and Time Pay in Auto Dealer Repair Shops', *Monthly Labor Review*, September 1975, pp. 45–6.

Kirzner, Israel M., *Competition and Entrepreneurship* (Chicago: University of Illinois Press, 1973).

Kirzner, Israel M., *Discovery and the Capitalist Process* (Chicago: University of Chicago Press, 1985).

Knight, Frank H., *Risk, Uncertainty and Profit* (New York: Harper, Torch Books, 1921/1965).

Kornai, Janos, *Anti-Equilibrium* (Amsterdam: North-Holland Publishing Co., 1971).

Kramer, Jerry, *Distant Replay* (New York: Putnam, 1985).

Kristol, Irving, *Two Cheers for Capitalism* (New York: Basic Books, 1978).

Kuznets, Simon, 'Two Centuries of Economic Growth: Reflections on U.S. Experience', *The American Economic Review*, February 1977.

Lancaster, Tony and Chesher, Andrew, 'An Econometric Analysis of Reservation Wages', *Econometrica*, November 1983, pp. 1661–76.

Landes, David, S., *Revolution in Time* (Cambridge, Mass.: Harvard University Press, 1983).

Landsberger, Michael, 'An Integrated Model of Consumption and Market Activity: The Children Effect', *Proceedings of the American Statistical Association*, 1971, pp. 137–42.

Lane, Frederick C., *Venice: A Maritime Republic* (Baltimore: Johns Hopkins, 1973).

Latane, Bibb, Williams, Kipling and Harkins, Stephen, 'Many Hands Make Light the Work: The Causes and Consequences of Social Loafing', *Journal of Personality and Social Psychology*, 37, 1979, pp. 822–32. Reference from Maital, 1981.

Laumas, G. S. and Ram, Rati, 'Role of Wealth in Consumption: An Empirical Investigation', *The Review of Economics and Statistics*, May 1982, pp. 204–10.

Leamer, Edward E., 'Let's Take the Con Out of Econometrics', *American Economic Review*, 73, March 1983, pp. 31–43.

Leff, Nathanial H., 'Dependency Rates and Savings Rates: A New Look', in J. Simon and J. DaVanzo, eds, *Research in Population Economics*, vol. 2, (Greenwich: JAI Press, 1980).

Leibenstein, Harvey, *Beyond Economic Man* (Cambridge, Mass.: Harvard University Press, 1976).

Leontief, Wassily, *Essays in Economics* (New York: Oxford University Press, 1966).

Leontief, Wassily, Letter titled 'Academic Economics', *Science*, vol. 217, 9 July 1982, p. 104.

Letwin, William, *The Origins of Scientific Economics*, (Garden City, NY: Doubleday Anchor Books, 1965).

Levy, Haim and Simon, Julian L., 'Choosing the Best Advertising Appropriation when Appropriations React Over Time', in Jagdish Sheth, ed., *Research in Marketing*, vol. I, (Greenwich: JAI Press, 1979).

Lindsey, Lawrence B., 'Lessons of the 1981 Tax Cut', *Wall Street Journal*, 6 May 1986, p. 26.

Lock, E. A., Feren, D. B., McCaleb, V. M., Shaw, K. N. and Dermy, A. T., 'The Relative Effectiveness of Four Methods of Motivating Employee Performance', in K. D. Dunction, M. M. Gruneberg and D. Wallis, *Changes in Working Life* (New York: John Wiley, 1980).

Lupton, Tom and Cunnison, Sheila, 'The Cash Reward for an Hour's Work Under Three Piecework Incentive Systems', *Manchester School of Econ-*

omics and Social Studies, 1957, p. 269.

Machlup, Fritz, *Essays in Economics Semantics* (New York: Norton, 1967).

Maital, Shlomo, *Minds, Markets, and Money* (New York: Basic Books, 1982).

Mandelbaum, David G., ed., *Selected Writings of Edward Sapir in Language, Culture and Personality* (Berkeley, Cal.: University of California Press, 1963).

Mandeville, Bernard, *The Fable of the Bees* (New York: Capricorn Books, 1705/1962).

Markowitz, Harry, 'The Utility of Wealth', *Journal of Political Economy*, vol. 60, 1952.

Marshall, Alfred, *Principles of Economies* (London: Macmillan, 1920).

Mayer, Thomas, *Permanent Income, Wealth, and Consumption* (Berkeley: University of California Press, 1972).

McClelland, David C., *The Achieving Society* (Princeton: Von Nostrand, 1961).

McDermott, John J., *The Philosophy of John Dewey: The Structure of Experience*, (New York: Putnams, 1973).

McNeill, William H., *The Rise of the West* (New York: Mentor, 1963) pp. 56 ff.

McNeill, William H., *The Human Condition* (Princeton: Princeton University Press, 1980).

Mellor, John W., 'The Use and Productivity of Farm Family Labor in Early Stages of Agricultural Growth', *Journal of Farm Economics*, 1963, pp. 517–34.

Menger, Carl, *Principles of Economics* (New York: New York University Press, 1871/1981).

Modigliani, Franco, 'The Life Cycle Hypothesis of Saving, The Demand for Wealth, and the Supply of Capital', *Social Research*, vol. 33, Summer 1966, pp. 160–217.

Mosher, Steven W., *Broken Earth: The Rural Chinese* (New York: The Free Press, 1983).

Murray, Charles, *Losing Ground* (New York: Manhattan Institute, 1984).

Myrdal, Gunnar, *Asian Drama*, vol. 1 (New York: Pantheon, 1968).

Nair, Kusum, *Blossoms in the Dust* (New York: Praeger, 1962).

Nef, John V., *Western Civilization Since the Renaissance* (New York: Harper and Row, 1950/1963).

New York Times, 31 October 1982, p. 24F.

Newsweek, 7 February 1983, p. 46.

Novak, Michael, *The Spirit of Democratic Capitalism* (New York: Simon and Schuster, 1981).

O'Boyle, Thomas F., 'High Cost of Liquidation Keeping Some Money-Losing Plants Open', *Wall Street Journal*, 29 November 1982, p. 23.

Olson, Mancur, *The Decline of Nations* (New Haven: Yale University Press, 1982).

Patinkin, Don, *Money, Interest, and Prices* (New York: Harper and Row, 1965).

Patton, John A., 'High Wages Don't Necessarily Mean High Costs', *Wall Street Journal*, 8 October 1982, p. 22.

Pencavel, John H., 'Work Effort, On-the-Job Screening, and Alternative Methods of Renumeration', in Ronald G. Ehrenberg, ed., *Research in Labor Economics*, vol. 1 (Greenwich, Conn.: JAI Press, 1977), pp. 225–58.

Perella, Vera C., 'Moonlighters: Their Motivations and Characteristics', *Monthly Labor Review*, 1970, pp. 57–64.

Phelps, Edmund S., 'Population Increase', *Canadian Journal of Economics*, 1968, pp. 497–518.

Pingali, Prabhu and Binswanger, Hans, 'Population Density and Family Systems: The Changing Locus of Innovations and Technical Change', IUSSP Paper, 15–18 December 1984.

Popper, Karl, *Unended Quest* (LaSalle, Illinois: Open Court Publishing Co., 1974/76).

Possony, Stefan T., ed., *The Lenin Reader* (Chicago: Regnery, 1966) p. 208.

Preston, Lee E. and Collins, Norman R., 'Studies in a Simulated Market', *Institute of Business and Economic Research*, Berkeley, CA, 1966.

Primeaux, Walter J., 'An Assessment of X-Efficiency Gained Through Competition', *Review of Economics and Statistics*, vol. lxiii, no. 1 (Winter 1983), pp. 32–4.

Ram, Rati, 'Dependency Rates and Aggregate Savings: A New International Cross-Section Study', *American Economic Review*, vol. 72 (3), June 1982, pp. 537–44.

Ram, Rati, 'Dependency Rates and Savings: Reply', *American Economic Review*, 74 (1), March 1984, pp. 234–37.

Ram, Rati and Schultz, Theodore W., 'Life Span, Health, Savings, and Productivity', *Economic Development and Cultural Change*, April 1979, pp. 329–421.

Read, Herbert, *To Hell With Culture* (New York: Schocken Books, 1963).

Rees, Albert, *The Economics of Work and Pay*, 2nd edn (New York: Harper and Row, 1979).

Rees, Albert and Schultz, George P., *Workers and Wages in an Urban Labor Market* (Chicago: University of Chicago Press, 1970).

Ringelmann, quoted by Shlomo, Maital, *Minds, Markets, and Money* (New York: Basic Books, 1982), p. 126.

Rischin, M., ed., *The American Gospel of Success* (Chicago: Quadrangle Books, 1965).

Robinson, Joan, 'The Production Function and the Theory of Capital', in

Collected Economic Papers, vol. 2, Blackwell, 1965, pp. 114–31. First published in *Review of Economic Studies*, vol. 21, 1953–4, pp. 81–106.

Robinson, Joan, 'What Are the Questions?', *The Journal of Economic Literature*, vol. xv, no. 4, December 1977, pp. 1318–73.

Rothe, Harold F., 'Output Rates Among Chocolate Dippers', *Journal Of Applied Psychology*, April 1951, p. 96, and see earlier publications cited there.

Ryan, Thomas A., *Work and Effort*, (New York: Ronald, 1947).

Samuelson, Paul, 'Economists and the History of Ideas', *American Economic Review*, L11, March 1962, pp. 1–18.

Samuelson, Robert J., 'Busting the U.S. Budget: The Cost of an Aging American', *National Journal*, 18 February 1978.

Sanger, Margaret, *An Autobiography* (New York: Dover Publications, Inc., 1938).

Schelling, Thomas C., *The Strategy of Conflict* (Cambridge, Mass.: Harvard University Press, 1960).

Scherer, Frederick M., 'Demand Pull and Technological Invention: Schmookler Revisited', *The Journal of Industrial Economics*, xxx, March 1982, pp. 225–37.

Scherer, Frederick M., *Industrial Market Structure and Economic Performance* (Chicago: Rand McNally, 1970).

Schlaifer, Robert, 'The Relay Assembly Test Room: An Alternative Statistical Interpretation', *American Sociological Review*, vol. 45, no. 6, December 1980, pp. 995–1005.

Schmalensee, Richard, 'A Model of Promotional Competition in Oligopoly', *Review of Economic Studies*, vol. 43, 1976, pp. 493–507.

Schmookler, Jacob, *Invention and Economic Growth* (Cambridge, Mass.: Harvard University Press, 1966).

Schultz, Theodore W., 'The Value of the Ability to Deal with Disequilibria', *Journal of Economic Literature*, 1975, pp. 827–46.

Schultz, Theodore W., 'Investment in Entrepreneurial Ability', *Scandinavian Journal of Economics*, December 1980.

Schumpeter, Joseph A., *Capitalism, Socialism and Democracy* (New York: Harper Torchbooks, 1942/1950).

Scully, John J., 'The Influence of Family Size on Efficiency within the Farm – An Irish Study', *The Journal of Agricultural Economics*, 1962, pp. 116–21.

Seiler, Eric, 'Piece Rate vs. Time Rate: The Effect of Incentives on Earnings', *The Review of Economics and Statistics*, August 1984, pp. 363–76.

Selvin, Hanan and Hagstrom, Warren O., 'The Empirical Classification of Formal Groups', *American Social Review*, June 1963, pp. 298–308.

Sen, Amartya K., 'Peasants and Dualism With or Without Surplus Labor', *Journal of Political Economy*, vol. 74, 1966, pp.   5–50.

Shaffer, J. D., 'Information About Price and Income Elasticity for Food Obtained for Survey Data', *Journal of Farm Economics*, vol. 73, October 1965, pp. 536–9.

Shefrin, H. M. and Thaler, Richard, 'Life Cycle vs. Self-Control Theories of Saving: A Look at the Evidence', paper presented at the Econometric Society Meetings, San Francisco, December 1983.

Shelton, John P., 'Allocative Efficiency *vs.* "X-Efficiency": Comment', *The American Economic Review*, December 1987.

Shisko, Robert and Rostker, Bernard, 'The Economics of Multiple Job Holding', *American Economic Review*, vol. 66, June 1976, pp. 298–308.

Shubik, Martin, *Strategy and Market Structure*, (New York: John Wiley and Sons, 1959).

Silva, John M. III, 'Psychological Aspects of Elite Long-Distance Running', *National Forum*, vol. lxiii, no. 1 (Winter 1983), pp. 32–4.

Simon, Edelgard, 'A Changing German Attitude Toward Work', *Wall Street Journal*, 15 December 1982, p. 27.

Simon, Herbert A., *The Sciences of the Artificial*, 2nd edn (Cambridge, Mass.: The MIT Press, 1981).

Simon, Julian L., *Issues in the Economics of Advertising* (Urbana: University of Illinois Press, 1970).

Simon, Julian L., *The Management of Advertising* (Englewood Cliffs: Prentice-Hall, 1971).

Simon, Julian L., *Applied Managerial Economics* (Englewood Cliffs: Prentice-Hall, 1975).

Simon, Julian L., *The Economics of Population Growth* (Princeton: Princeton University Press, 1977), p. 60.

Simon, Julian L., *The Ultimate Resource* (Princeton: Princeton University Press: 1981).

Simon, Julian L., 'Are There Economies of Scale in Advertising?', *Journal of Advertising Research*, vol. 5, June 1965, pp. 15–19.

Simon, Julian L., 'The Cause of the Newspaper Rate Differential: A Subjective-Demand-Curve Differential', *Journal of Political Economy*, October 1965, pp. 536–9.

Simon, Julian L., 'The Economic Effect of State Monopoly of Packaged Liquor Retailing', *Journal of Political Economy*, April 1966, pp. 188–94.

Simon, Julian L., 'The Effect of Competitive Structure Upon Advertising Expenditures', *Quarterly Journal of Economics*, vol. lxxxi, November 1967, pp. 610–27.

Simon, Julian L., 'The Effect of Income on Suicide', *American Journal of Sociology*, vol. 74, 1968, pp. 302–3.

Simon, Julian L., 'A Further Test of the Kinky Oligopoly Demand Curve', *American Economic Review*, December 1969, pp. 971–5.

Simon, Julian L., 'Interpersonal Comparisons Can Be Made – And Used for Redistribution Decisions', *Kyklos*, vol. xxvii, no. 1, 1974, pp. 63–98.

Simon, Julian L., 'Firm Size and Market Behavior', mimeo, 1982.

Simon, Julian L., *The Economic Consequences of Immigration* (Oxford: Blackwell, forthcoming).

Simon, Julian L. and Arndt, Johan, 'The Shape of the Advertising Response Function', *Journal of Advertising Research*, 20 August 1980, pp. 11–30.

Simon, Julian L. and Barnes, Carl B., 'The Middle-Class U.S. Consumption Function: A Hypothetical-Question Study of Expected Consumer Behavior', *Bulletin of the Oxford Institute of Economics and Statistics*, February 1970, pp. 73–80.

Simon, Julian L. and Ben-Ur, Joseph, 'The Advertising Budget's Determinants in a Market with Two Competing Firms', *Management Science*, vol. 28, May 1982, pp. 500–19.

Simon, Julian L. and Golembo, Leslie, 'The Spread of a Cost-Free Business Innovation: The Case of the January White Sale', *Journal of Business*, October 1967, pp. 385–8.

Simon, Julian L. and Pilarski, Pilarski, Adam M., 'The Effect of Population Growth Upon the Quantity of Education Children Receive', *Review of Economics and Statistics*, vol. 61, 1979, pp. 572–84.

Simon, Julian L., Puig, Carlos and Aschoff, John, 'Duopoly Simulations and Theory: An End to Cournot', *The Review of Economic Studies*, vol. xl, 1973, pp. 353–66.

Simon, Julian L. and Rashid, Salim 'The Effect of Numbers Upon Competitive Effort', 1986, xeroxed.

Simon, Rita and Simon, Julian, L., 'Class, Status, and Savings By Negroes', *American Sociologist*, August 1968 pp. 218–9.

Slutsky, Eugen E., 'On the Theory of the Budget of the Consumer', in K. E. Boulding and G. J. Stigler, eds, *Readings in Price Theory*, (Homewood: Irwin, 1951).

Smith, Adam, *An Inquiry into the Nature and Causes of the Wealth of Nations* (Chicago: University of Chicago Press, 1776/1976).

Smith, James P., 'Assets, Savings, and Labor Supply', *Economic Inquiry*, vol. xv, no. 4, 1977.

Smith, Vernon K., Williams, Arlington W., Bratton, W. Kenneth and Vannona, Michael G., 'Competitive Market Distinctions: Double Auctions vs. Sealed Bid-Offer Auctions', *American Economic Review*, 72, March 1982, pp. 55–77.

Snow, C.P., 'On Albert Einstein', *Commentary*, 613, March 1967, pp. 45–55.

Stafford, Frank P. and Cohen, Malcolm S., 'A Model of Work Effort and Productive Consumption', *Journal of Economic Theory*, 7, 1974, pp. 333–47.

Stevens, S. S., 'Measurement, Psychophysics, and Utility', in C. W. Churchman and Philburn Ratoosh, eds, *Measurement: Definitions and Theories* (New York: Wiley, 1959), pp. 18–63.

Stigler, George, 'Competition', *International Encyclopedia of the Social Sciences*, 3, 1968, p. 181.

Stigler, George J., 'A Theory of Oligopoly', *Journal of Political Economy*, 72, February 1964, pp. 44–61.

Stigler, George J., *Essays in the History of Economics* (Chicago: University of Chicago Press, 1965).

Stigler, George J., 'Price and Nonprice Competition', *Journal of Political Economy*, lxii, February 1964. Reprinted in *The Organization of Industry* (Homewood: Irwin, 1968).

Stys, W., 'The Influence of Economic Conditions on the Fertility of Peasant Women', *Population Studies*, 11, 1957, pp. 136–48.

Tarbell, Ida M., ed., *Selections from the Letters, Speeches, and State Papers of Abraham Lincoln* (Boston: Ginn and Co., 1911).

Terborg, James R. and Miller, Howard E., 'Motivation, Behavior, and Performance', *Journal of Applied Psychology*, vol. 63, 1978, pp. 29–39.

Tiffin, J., *Industrial Psychology*, (New York: Prentice Hall, 1942).

Tomer, John F., 'Worker Motivation: A Neglected Element in Micro-Micro Theory', *Journal of Economic Issues*, June 1981, vol. 15, no. 2, pp. 351–62.

Toynbee, Arnold J., *A Study of History: The Genesis of Civilizations, Part Two* (New York: Oxford University Press, 1962) vol. 2, p. 259.

Veblen, Thorstein, *The Theory of the Leisure Class* (New York: Mentor, 1890/1953), p. 137.

Viteles, Morris, *Industrial Psychology*, (New York: W. W. Norton and Company, 1932).

Von Mises, Ludwig, *Notes and Recollections*, (South Holland, Ill.: Libertarian Press, 1978).

Von Neumann, John and Morgenstern, Oskan, *Theory of Games and Economic Behavior*, 2nd edn (Princeton: Princeton University Press, 1947).

Von Thunen, Johann H., *The Isolated State* (New York: Pergamon, 1966).

Wall Street Journal, 'Labor Letter', 19 May, 1981, p. 1.

Wall Street Journal, 'Some Japanese Balk at Overseas Jobs', 9 July 1982, p. 14.

Wall Street Journal, 26 August 1982, p. 1.

Wall Street Journal, 30 September 1982, p. 1.

Wall Street Journal, 'Limited Inc's Initial Steps Slow Profit in Revitalizing Lane Bryant Division', 12 October 1982, p. 24.

Wall Street Journal, 'Many Plant Closings Reflect Switch in Strategy as Well as Poor Economy', 15 October 1982, p. 29.

Wall Street Journal 20 October 1982, p. 16.

Wall Street Journal, 'Swiss Still the Thriftiest, With $14,122 Salted Away', 1

November 1982, p. 34.

Wall Street Journal 'A Revolutionary Way to Streamline the Factory', 15 November 1982, editorial page.

Wall Street Journal, 9 May 1983, p. 1.

Wall Street Journal, 'No Help Wanted', 11 May 1983, p. 22.

Wall Street Journal, 'Ohio Firm Relies on Incentive-Pay System to Motivate Workers and Maintain Profits', 12 August 1983, p. 15.

Wall Street Journal, 'Unions Say Auto Firms Use Interplant Rivalry to Raise Work Quotas', 7 November 1983, p. 1.

Wall Street Journal, 'Francisco Rodriguez Earns a Living Driving in Latin War Zone', 16 December 1983, p. 1.

Wall Street Journal, 'Executives See Some Benefits in Recession', 13 January 1984, p. 1.

Wall Street Journal, 'Crow Indians Find Huge Coal Reserves Help Them Very Little', 31 January 1984, p. 25.

Wall Street Journal, 'Streamlined Smokestack Industries Are Beginning to Show Big Profits', 28 March 1984, p. 35.

Wall Street Journal, 'Great Productivity At a Utah Coal Mine Is Called "God's Plan"', 12 April 1984, p. 1.

Wall Street Journal, 'Major Oil Firms Are Slashing Jobs As Takeovers Rise, Demand Sags', 19 April 1984, p. 33.

Wall Street Journal, 'Japan Considering Plan to Shorten Workweek', 30 August 1984, p. 22.

Wall Street Journal, 'Florida in Winter Is No Vacation for a Cane Cutter', 3 January 1985, p. 1.

Wall Street Journal, 'At 'Scrub U.', GM's Janitors Learn Latest Ways to Get the Dirt Out', 21 May 1985, p. 33.

Wall Street Journal, 'A Panel of European Business Executives Sees Narrowing of Gap with U.S., Japan', 26 June 1985, p. 30.

Wall Street Journal, 'Back to Piecework: More Companies Want to Base Pay Increases on the Output of Their Employees', 15 November 1985, p. 15.

Wan, Henry Y., Jr., *Economic Growth* (New York: Harcourt Brace, Jovanovich, 1973).

Washington Post, 'Vietnamese Shrimpers Alter Texas Gulf Towns', 1984, pp. A1, A6.

Washington Post, 'Where Anglos Fear to Tread', 6 March 1984, p. C11.

Washington Post, 'The Painful Downsizing of AT&T', 2 September 1984, p. G1.

Washington Post, '10 Paroled Felons Quit Work-Release Jobs', 16 April 1985, pp. A1 and A11.

Washington Post, 23 October 1985, p. C-2.

Weber, James A., *Grow or Die!* (New Rochelle, NY: Arlington House, 1977).

Weber, Max, *General Economic History* (New York: Collier Books, 1961).

Weinstein, Alan G. and Holzbach, Robert L. Jr., 'Impact of Individual Differences, Reward Distribution, and Task Structure on Productivity in a Simulated Work Environment', *Journal of Applied Psychology*, 58, December 1973.

White, Lynn, Jr., 'The Historical Roots of Our Ecologic Crisis', *Science*, vol. 155, no. 3767, 10 March 1967, p. 1203.

Wilensky, Harold, 'The Moonlighter: A Product of Relative Deprivation', *Industrial Relations*, vol. 3, 1963, pp. 105–24.

Wilson, Robert W., Ashton, Peter K. and Egon, Thomas P., *Innovation, Competition, and Government Policy in the Semiconductor Industry* (Lexington, Mass.: Lexington Books, 1980).

Winston, Gordon C., 'An International Comparison of Income and Hours of Work', *Review of Economics and Statistics*, vol. 48, 1966, pp. 28–39.

Yergin, Daniel, 'Awaiting the Next Oil Crisis', *New York Times Magazine*, 11 July 1982, p. 56.

Yotopoulos, Pan A. and Lau, Lawrence J., 'On Modeling the Agricultural Sector in Developing Economies: An Integrated Approach of Micro and Macro-Economics', *Journal of Development Economics*, 1974, pp. 105–27.

Index

Index by *Ann Barham*

DATE DUE

DEMCO 38-297